COMMERCIAL SPACE

Bars, Hotels and Restaurants

COMMERCIAL SPACE

Bars, Hotels and Restaurants

RotoVision SA

AUTHOR
Francisco Asensio Cerver

EDITOR IN CHIEF
Paco Asensio

PROJECT COORDINATOR
Rosa Maria Prats

PROOFREADING
Carola Moreno
A.B.C. Traduccions

TRANSLATION
A.B.C. Traduccions

© Copyright for International Edition
AXIS BOOKS, S.A.

© Copyright for English Edition
ROTOVISION S.A.
9 Route Suisse
CH-1295 Mies
Switzerland
Tel: 41-22-755 3055
Fax: 41-22-755 4072

ISBN: 2-88046-226-6

Printed in Singapore

It is undeniable that during the last two decades of the 20th Century public spaces have become recognised as stimulating centres for social relationships. The reasons behind the increase in this type of premises must be sought, not only, in a determined socio-economic situation, but also in a certain ideological philosophy, brought about by a sense of inevitable ambiguity that goes hand in hand with the close of the century. What has become known as "the culture of the image" dictates all of the activities of the individual who, as a social being, needs such spaces as a backdrop to his encounters, relationships and the pursuit of leisure.

This cult, of the physical appearance of the individual, has been carried over into his vital environment and has become manifest in all of the spaces around which his existence is organised: the private (his home), the semi-private (his place of work), and the public leisure spaces to which this present volume is dedicated. This process has been transformed into the concept of environmental atmospheres, a concept which stands as equally true for all three sections of the above classification. This same period has been witness to a spectacular flowering of interior design which has also touched the different environments of our domestic, professional and recreational life.

There are three kinds of public spaces, within the area of recreational life, which can be considered as the temples of contemporary social relationships: bars and discotheques, restaurants, and hotels. The two main aims of this present introduction consist in analyzing the principal characteristics of these three groups and in presenting some of the projects featured in this present volume to exemplify the variety and plurality of these spaces.

The first section for analysis refers to discotheques and bars with a musical environment. In these spaces the designers have been able to give free rein to their imagination and to display the full range of their creative talent in the search for originality and the assault on the limits of the possible. However in certain instances this headlong flight from mediocrity has resulted in excesses which, in the name of post-modernism, have done little justice to the fundamental principles of pragmatism and functional logic.

The present volume offers examples of bars and discotheques which have brilliantly interwoven the most innovative audacities of interior design with high standards of comfort and functionality in relation to the space and the services that are defined by that space. It is enough in this context to mention Petrus, the project in which Peter Leonard Associates have embodied a singularly American concept of luxury; the Kix Bar, a sensual cross fertilisation of the architectural and the pictorial; and Barna Crossing, an ambitious project which summarises all of the disparate elements of the conceptual philosophy of contemporary leisure.

In the restaurants section which includes, both those places exclusively destined for the exercise of the gastronomic arts, and also multifunctional premises which include this aspect as one element of a space offering a range of leisure activities. An outstanding example of the former is Beddington's Restaurant, a project in which the Baroque and biomporphic language of Borek Sipek has succeeded in achieving a transformation of the spatial atmosphere without resorting to the excesses of nihilistic design; and the Kabuto restaurant, in which Iavicoli & Rossi have experimented with the difficult terrain of an intercultural marriage between Eastern and Western icons.

Among the multi-functional premises featured in this volume centre stage is taken by two singular projects: Teatriz, a work in which Philippe Stark was able to control all aspects of the planning and design work, once again confirming his capacity to handle any type of creative project; and Taxim Nightpark, a project in which Branson & Coates have championed a blend of cultural influences from what is, without doubt, the most unusual of perspectives.

Finally the section corresponding to hotels, an area which in recent years has undergone a renovation of concepts in order to adapt to present day strategies of supply and demand. This revision has been produced, both from an aesthetic, and also from a functional, perspective: in the first the design of the spaces has found expression through the latest and most innovative trends in interior design; while in the second, the importance of the contemporary role of the hotel lobby as a social and cultural meeting places has been given its due. In this context, again, it is enough to mention the diversity of the facilities offered by the Il Palazzo Hotel, a multi-disciplinary project to which many of the most creative designers from the East and the West have lent their considerable talent. This, however, is only one example of the rich variety of proposals which can be found in this present volume, in which the attempt has been made to illustrate the effervescent plurality which has come to define the creative impulse behind contemporary public spaces.

BARS

HOTELS

RESTAURANTS

Bars

PETRUS

Peter Leonard Associates

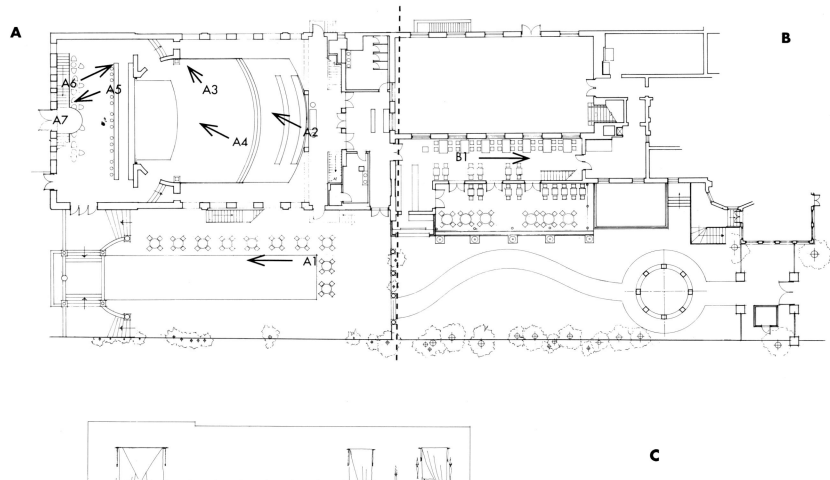

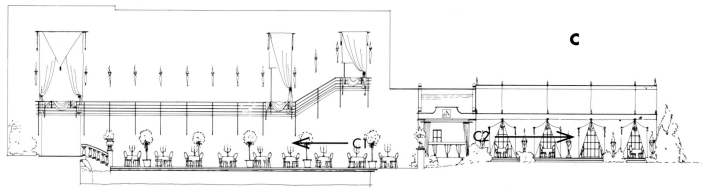

Floor plan of the premises, laid out in sections.

Elevation section.

Above, a view of the illuminated fountain-pool, with the bridge in the background. (A1, C1)

A view of the old stalls area from the upper floor, showing the original circle and the slightly arched ceiling, with classical and opulent multicoloured forms drawn in purple, golden and white tones. (A2)

The remodelling of a women's club in Atlanta (USA) converting it into a fashionable night club, is one of the most original and creative pieces of work to have come from the practice directed by Peter Leonard.

Peter Leonard Associates was established in 1981, and is sustained by the work of a team of more than 30 people with a trajectory endorsed through projects commissioned by a highly select clientele. The work of Peter Leonard Associates includes the interior design of a whole range of shops, commercial and leisure spaces, and graphics. Peter Leonard came to international recognition through the Virgin Megastore project in Paris which opened the doors to a success which was consolidated by work on the Science Museum in London, Laura Ashley's Mother & Child and the Abbey Road Studios, among others. In 1986 Peter Leonard founded the firm Soho Design, creating a new type of furniture inspired in the forms of the past yet manufactured using present day techniques and materials. Their furniture collections, as well as their interior design, currently enjoy a great deal of success in Europe, Japan and North America.

This project by Peter Leonard was based on an old twenties building which had originally been a theatre and had later been converted

A partial view of the dance floor, showing the location of the sound systems at the sides. The deep red heavy curtains with their yellow pattern, reminiscent of the theatre, can be seen hanging in the background. (A3)

A view of the restaurant in the corridor which links the two
interior spaces of the building. (B1, C2)

into a women's club, this latter being the promoter of the present project, which was finished in July 1989. The run down state of the
structure called for an in depth rehabilitation
in which the architect, as far as possible, con-
served the original brick skeleton and the
markedly scenographic spatial distribution.
The aim was to take advantage of this pre-
existing structure in order to establish an
expressive dialogue between the old and the
new and, at the same time, to organise the different spaces by means of a rational system
which would link them in a pliant and natural
manner. An aesthetic language was used
which with great plasticity combined the style
of the old Hollywood with concepts of luxury
and extravagance proper to American culture.

A view of the seating area located in the old circle.

On this page and the following, a panoramic view of the
dancing area and the bar, with the bar counter and a seating
area. Between the two sections the large separating proscenium arch can be seen, decorated with an intense colour
scheme of purple, golden and white tones. The central area
of the arch is completely glazed. (A4)

A partial view of the bar counter and the bar seating area with the Soho furnishings expressly designed for Petrus. (A5)

View of the bar counter in the area of the wings of the old theatre. The whole area is in visual contact with the dance floor through the glass of the arch separating the stage and the wings. (A6)

Through this combination an essentially theatrical result was achieved which was perfectly adapted to the recreational activities for which the premises were intended.

The aesthetic and functional possibilities of the exterior areas were strengthened, establishing a space where water and vegetation were the most important visual components. The adjoining land on the left hand side of the building was divided into two differentiated areas. The first would be the entrance with an approaching pathway flanked by trees and gardens and a circular fountain a few feet from the doorway itself. The second section hinges on a fountain-pool with central illumination around which two lines of tables are placed leading to a type of bridge which is integrated into the architecture of the building, spanning the water and approached by wide and elegant stairways.

The interior space was divided into two volumes which were based on the structures of the old theatre and the women's club. The first amply and harmoniously proportioned was the ideal section for the installation of the dance floor, with a bar and a seating area, the whole being given a spectacular and attractive aesthetic treatment. The second section kept its original use and the restaurant were located in the corridor linking the two spaces. Here more stylised and sober criteria was employed where the mellow tones of the colour scheme, the contrast between natural and artificial light and the comfortable furnishings, contribute to the creation of an atmosphere which is both intimate and relaxed.

The connection between interior and exterior, the contrast of ornamentation, the combination of colours and atmospheres in each specific area and the voluptuous character which predominates throughout the decoration of the premises contribute to the definition of a style emanating ostentation and extravagance and closely identified with the American concept of luxury. The creation of a heterogenous aesthetic language was definitive in the achievement

of this objective, wherein multiple references are combined ranging from the Imperial style to the golden age of Hollywood. Peter Leonard has once again demonstrated his ability in the treatment and perception of space and his talent for recreating suggestive and, at the same time functional, atmospheres on the basis of pre-established structures and models.

Different perspectives of the small semicircular elevated floor opposite the bar counter which can be reached by steel stairs sheathed in bronze. (A7)

BAR MADDALENA

King Kong Production

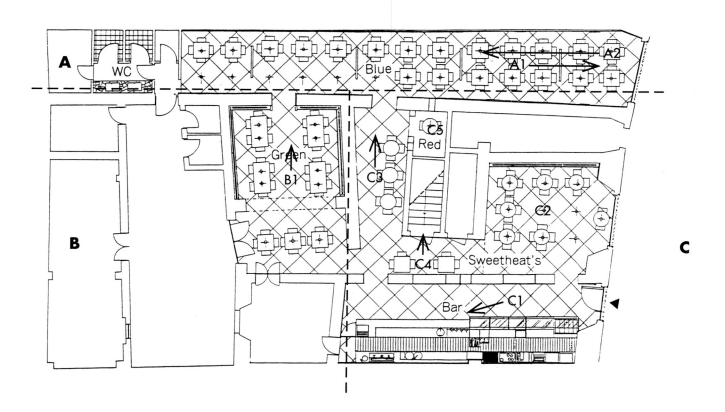

Floor plan of the Maddalena Bar and distribution of the different spaces.

A partial view of the entrance to the premises, with the black granite bar counter in the background and the vaulted plaster canopy which serves as a screen, onto which the bar's logo is projected. (C1)

Stefano Giovannoni and Guido Venturini are the two founder members of the innovative King Kong Productions Studio, which they set up in 1985 with the aim of working in an experimental avant-garde manner in the field of design, interior decoration and architecture. They take their inspiration from fantasy, cinematographic mythology and the territory of the imaginary and artificial fiction, using icons which express a double meaning that is both poetic and ironic. They have exhibited their work in many prestigious Italian and international shows including the Biennials in Paris (1982), Venice and Barcelona (1985), the Atelier Nouveau in Tokyo (1986), the Milan Triennial and the Sao Paolo Biennial, both in 1987. Examples of their work are on permanent exhibition at the George Pompidou centre in Paris.

One of King Kong Productions' most strongly expressive projects was the Maddalena Bar built in 1989 in Prato, a town in the north of Italy. This bar, called the Loveburger by its designers, is a space which attempts to break down cultural, tribal and economic barriers for the price of a simple hamburger and to promote new kinds of leisure activity through an environment that is both excessive and suggestive.

Given the innovative and experimental character of the project the risk was obviously being run of a short life span once the novelty value had worn off. However both the architects and the developers decided to take on the challenge, without ruling out the possibility of

Above, a view of the black room with impersonal graphics on the walls dramatising sequences of a lovers troth in a tone which is both gentle and at the same time ironic. (C2)

A partial view of the black room, with a white skull on one wall, whose eyes have been replaced by hearts. This motif also appears in the centre of the tables throughout the premises, and has become the identifying symbol for the Maddalena Bar. (C2)

future modifications. The aesthetic and conceptual intention was to create a space with a series of atmospheres that would be capable of stimulating the public.

The surface area of the bar consists of one floor with a rectangular tendency which is divided into a series of rooms characterised by the use of different monochromatic tones in each room. Flooring and furnishings are the only elements which extend any kind of physical uniformity through the different spaces.

The area around the entrance is dominated by the location of the bar counter, a monolithic block cut out of black granite, over which a vaulted plaster canopy in blue tones, the most

Above and on the left, a perspective of the main corridor with the blue room at the end (C3). On the right, a view of the entrance to the private areas of the premises, in yellow. (C4)

The absence of doors leads to chromatic contrasts as in the photograph. (C3)

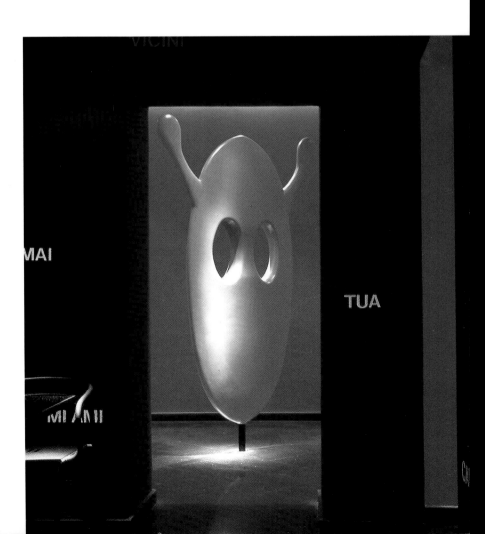

expressive detail of this initial area, is suspended. This entrance and service area is connected to the kitchen and the store which are both located at the back of the premises.

In continuation there is a room where black is the predominant colour and in which some of the general characteristics of the premises are illustrated: firstly the squared polished cement floor around which the coal coloured tables and chairs are distributed, then the artificial lighting based on built in spots and neon tubes, and finally the distribution of the music sound system designed by Dolfi of Florence.

A corridor provides access to the remaining spaces and links the different rooms. On the right there is a small red room with just one table and two chairs and with heart shaped varnished wooden plaques (also red) on the walls.

Opposite this small room another of the representative spaces of the premises can be found characterised by the use of a greenish tone and by the placing on the walls of oval plaques of varnished wood in a darker green. A rectangular opening leads through to the blue room provoking a chromatic disharmony of plastic implication. This juxtaposition is repeated through the different rooms giving rise to a sequence of vivid contrasts. The absence of doors emphasises the creation of these contrasts between the different coloured rooms which announce the entry into a universe which is absolutely distinct from that which preceded it. The blue room at the end of the passage is characterised by the presence

On this page and the following, overall view of the green room with the blue room in the background. (B1)

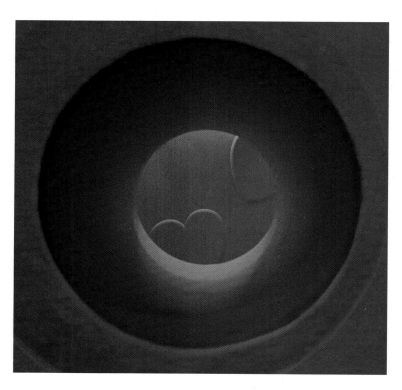

of three flat figures which through the use of curved lines and a special sheathing take on the appearance of ghosts in the form of masks, with all the ancestral and symbolic reminiscences which this may suggest to each individual. Another distinctive factor in this section is the lighting which consists of flexible tubes in which small points of light are located at regular intervals drawing the outlines of skulls and bones on the ceiling. The room as a whole has an unsettling feel capable of evoking a wide diversity of sensations through a treatment which oscillates between the recreational and the poetic.

To summarise, it is a risky and eclectic work, yet at the same time it achieves a brilliance that reflects the restless and avant-garde creative personality of its two designers.

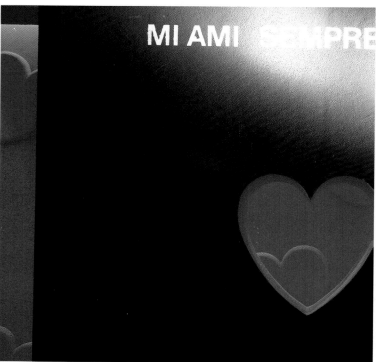

Chromatic contrasts caused by the openings which link the small red room with the other rooms which surround it.

A perspective of the same room showing its reduced dimensions. (C5)

On the previous page, a view of the blue room with the sculptural figures, by Sickens, presiding over the space (A1). On the right, another perspective of the same room (A2).

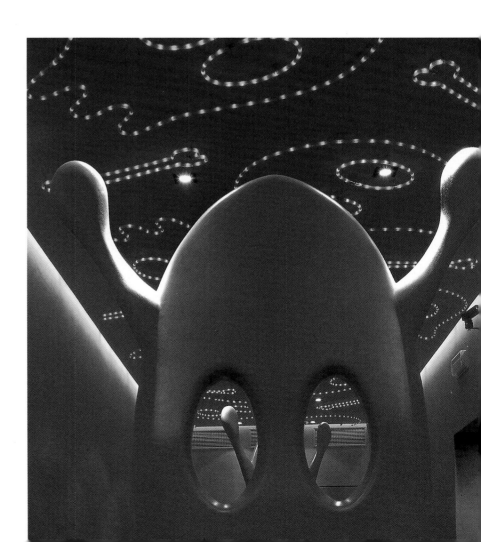

This photograph shows the lighting system used in this room with flexible tubes on which points of light are located drawing the outline of skulls and bones on the ceiling.

KIX BAR

Wolfgang Kaitna, Rüdiger Reichel & Kurt Smetana

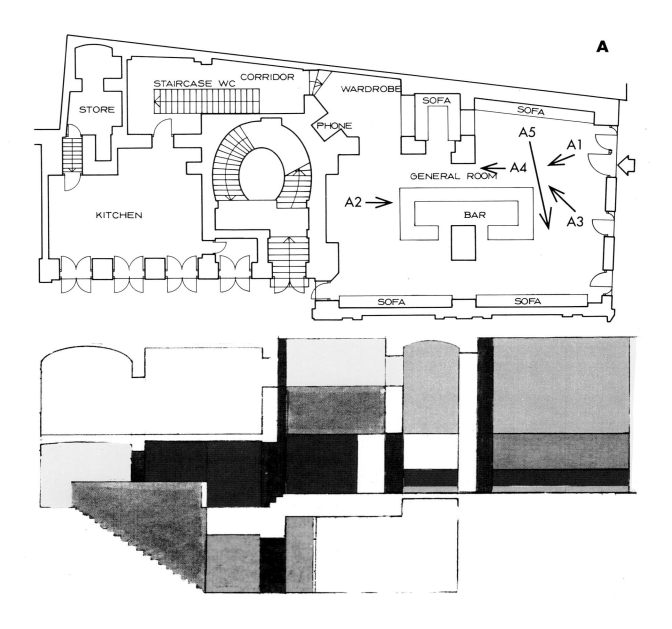

Floor plan of the premises (A). Below, distribution and colour scheme of the walls.

On the following page, a view of the bar counter in which the characteristic stools have been replaced by two rails for hands and feet, in wood and metal respectively. (A1)

Another perspective of the bar counter, showing the light emanating from the glazed surface emphasising its role as the vertebral axis of the space. (A2)

Elevation of part of the premises, showing the infinite sequence of individual framings which change as the situation of the spectator changes.

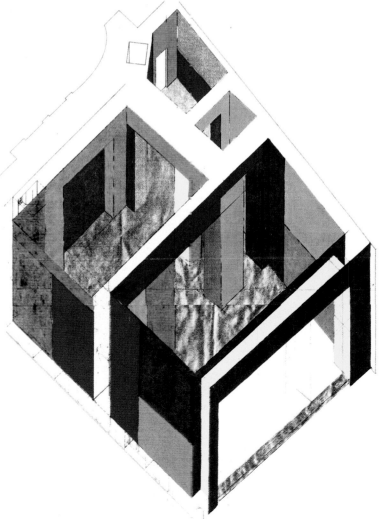

A view of one corner of the bar from the bar counter, on the right some of the furnishings, with the red benches fixed to the wall. These are the only elements which obstruct a direct view of the mural work. The absence of other decorative elements is a constant throughout the interior space. (A3)

In recent years few creative proposals in the field of interior design have resulted in work as original as the Kix Bar, situated in the Bäckerstrasse in Vienna. It was designed on the basis of a symbiosis of architecture and painting and is presented as the location for a variety of activities in a stimulating environment. It is ideal for having a drink and having fun but also serves as the setting for the exchange of ideas, for contemplation and for the acquisition of new experiences. The decision of the architects to integrate the work of the painter Oskar Putz into the architecture of the bar is a response to the desire to transform his paintings into the potential genesis for new ideas. The three architects of the Kix Bar, all of Austrian origin, have had similar wor-

On the previous page, another perspective of the bar, on the right the semi-hidden U-shaped red sofa behind which the cloakroom and a public telephone are located. (A4)

Different views of the pictorial work of Oskar Putz and of the infinite combinations of colours, which vary with the perspective.

king trajectories mainly in the field of urban planning and the restructuring and remodelling of old urban and rural centres.

The basis for this project was a two storey premises with a rectangular floor-plan divided in two by a wall. The main public area is inside the Bäckerstrasse entrance where there is a bar and tables and chairs. A small door leads to the second area of the ground floor containing the kitchen and the circular stairs leading to the first floor. Another stairway leads to the washrooms located on a lower level.

The three pure primary colours, blue, yellow and red, together with two of their complements, green and orange, are the aesthetic protagonists of these premises covering the surface area of the walls in a variety of com-

Different corners of the premises, illustrating the predominance of the three pure primary colours, blue, yellow and red, alongside two of their complements, green and orange, following on from each other in multiple combinations.

Angle of the bar where the narrow windows opening out onto the main façade in Bäckerstrasse are located. (A5)

binations.

The move from flat painting to working in three dimensions, as is the case with architectural design, results in an infinite sequence of individual framings which change as the situation and perspective of the spectator changes. The homogenous nature of the interior is presented as a combination of multiple pictorial planes created in order to act as a dynamic stimulus.

The furnishings are based on the same aesthetic lines, with the tables and chairs set up in disperse groups along the length of the walls and due to their skeletal metallic structure the eye is drawn to the surfaces, red for the chairs and blue for the tables.

The floor is of light grey metal sheeting, a neutral solution with the advantage that it does not interfere with the perception of the mural colour scheme. Low voltage fluorescent tubing was chosen for the lighting and bestows an indirect and diffuse light which allows Putz's work to be contemplated without distraction. A glowing white light emanates from the interior of the bar counter emphasising the role of this structure as the vertebral axis of the space.

In conclusion, the Kix Bar represents a complete novelty in the field of the interior design of leisure spaces, an absolutely original project which has been brilliantly designed by its three architects.

BARNA CROSSING

Alfredo Arribas & Miguel Morte

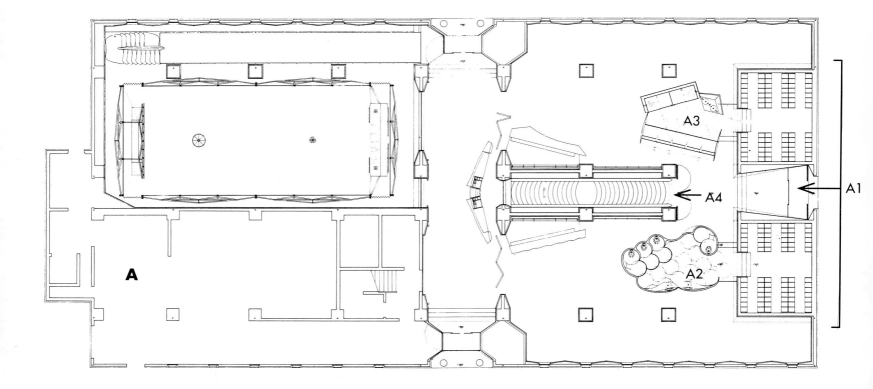

Floor plan of the ground floor at street level. (A)

On the following page, a view of the different levels of the premises seen from the dance area in the basement. (B1)

The key to an understanding of the creative process which has been adopted for this project is the use of the word crossing in the name; a crossing can be a link, a hybrid, or a union. These concepts are interpreted as enriching, representative of a uniting of complementary values that are never opposed. The objective was to achieve a union of cultures; of ideas, sensations and perceptions, a link between the different peoples and activities that are pertinent to the confusing close of this 20th century. The interpretation of this concept is manifested in a multi-usage space conceived in consonance with the new recreational habits and which goes much further than the simple concept of a macro-discotheque. The notion of dynamic space, in contrast to static and passive space, allowed for the comprehension of the idea which was the inspiration for Barna Crossing.

The project was put into the hands of Alfredo Arribas Associated Architects (AAAA) the prolific and internationally recognised Barcelona practice directed by Alfredo Arribas. Noteworthy examples among his recent work include the Escuela Elisava, The Velvet Bar, The Network Café (in collaboration with Eduard Samsó) and las Torres de Avila (with Mariscal), all in Barcelona. On the international stage The Harajuku Neones Café and Tokyo Time Power, both in Tokyo, The Manila Disco Europa, in

Access stairway to the basement where the dance area is located. (B2)

Tables and chairs in one of the bar areas next to the discotheque. (B5, C1)

Florence, and the Spanish Pavilion in Buchmesse, Frankfurt, must also be mentioned.

The project consisted of a design for the interior of a discotheque-bar-restaurant of 1,750 square metres, in Fukuoka, a city in Southern Japan. The premises are on the lower floors of a building by the Italian architect Aldo Rossi, which houses the Il Palazzo Hotel.

From the very beginning Arribas took on a team of collaborators, all from Barcelona, who helped him to complete all of the different design areas involved in the project: furniture, graphics, objects, decoration, wardrobe, music, kitchen, etc. Outstanding names in the world of design, such as Juli Capella, Quim Larrea, Chu Uroz, Alfonso Sostres, and Javier Mariscal, among others, actively participated in the work on Barna Crossing.

The architectural structure of this space conformed to the basic criteria of the macro-discotheque, divided into zones: a private club, discotheque, bars and restaurants; yet distanced from the conventional models for this type of premises, through a rejection of a rigid distribution of space in favour of an overall utilisation. Compartmentalisation was replaced by the creation of a kind of grand bazaar where it would be possible to experience and enjoy the various available activities together, thus encouraging new recreational and communicative habits.

Plans of the lower level of the premises, of the floor, and above, taking in the three hanging platforms which house the restaurant. (B)

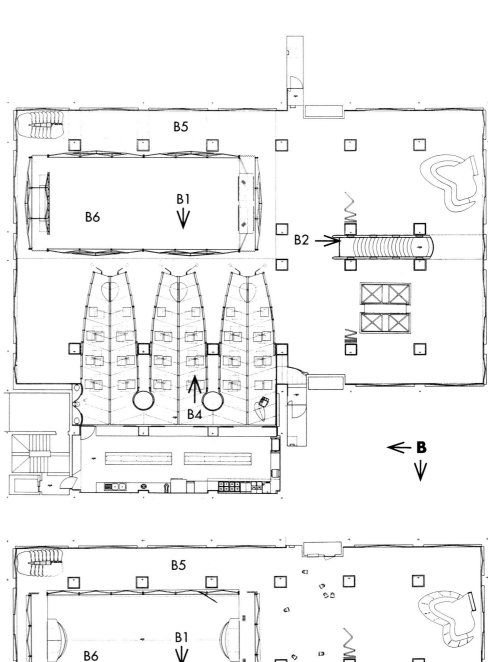

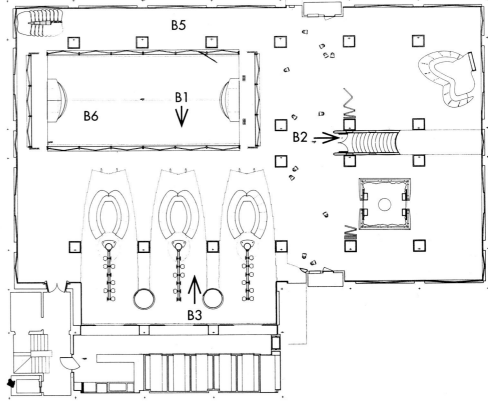

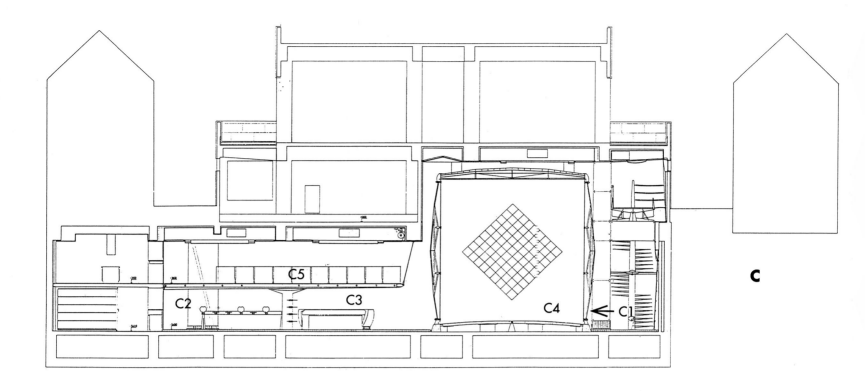

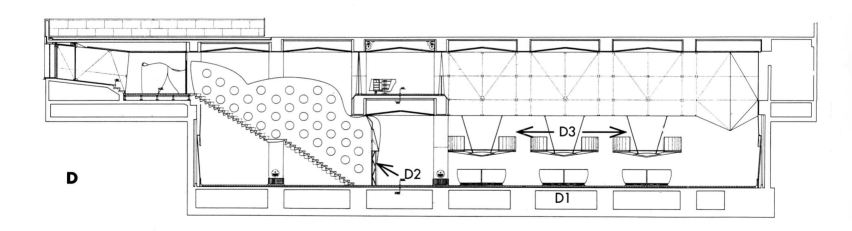

Section of the elevation of the basement and the mezzanine where the restaurant is located. (C). The plan below corresponds to the lengthways section of the same area. (D)

On the following page, exterior view of the building which houses Barna Crossing, with the entrance to the premises in the foreground. (A1)

The total space consists of 1,750 m², distributed over two floors, one at street level and the other in the basement. The floors presented a total height of 9 metres and included a mezzanine level of platforms on which the restaurant and kitchen were located.

Access from the street is at ground floor level, where there are a choice of entrances, the reception, the cloakroom and the washrooms, The Waiting Bar, The VIP Bar and a large open space featuring the glass box which acts as the discotheque. At the basement level there are three main bars, a fast food restaurant, The Ice Bar, The Vitamin Bar and the Glass Box discotheque. Despite this theoretical division the spaces are interrelated and the treatment that they were given, situates them all in close visual proximity.

The architectural intervention consisted of two main areas; the general work on the original structure of the building which houses the Barna Crossing space and which involved the installation of a large sheath or box which contains the premises; and the individual interventions on the different areas of the premises which constituted autonomous projects within the overall idea.

The strategy of housing the space inside a giant box was considered to be the ideal solu-

Above, perspective of the VIP Area where the Gaudí design furniture can be appreciated, with carpets by Elías Torres and Martínez Lapeña, and chairs by Mariscal. (A2)

Below, a view of The Waiting Bar with its curved bar counter on a luminous onyx veneer base, the furniture is by Oscar Tusquets. (A3)

Overall view of The Vitamin Bar with the sinuous forms of the counter presiding over the room. (C3)

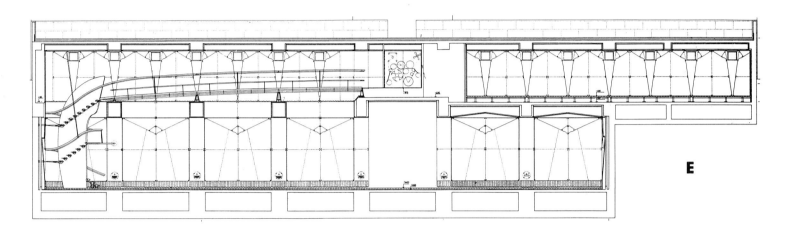

E

Section of the premises showing the lay-out of some of the technical installations. (E)

On the previous page, one of the three tongue shaped bars in the basement and one of the hanging platforms, on which the restaurant is located, can be seen above. (D1)

tion, in that it unified the space and made it homogenous. The sheathing also allowed for the concealment of the technical installations (electricity, air conditioning, lighting, sound, safety) and the acoustic and thermal insulation of the interior. Through the aluminium sheathing it was also possible to maintain the greatest respect for the order imposed by the architect of the building, Aldo Rossi, without having to renounce the design concepts for the interior of the premises.

A single floating floor, consisting of a combination of thick wooden boards, supports the whole of the interior sheathing. The presence of caissons in the ceiling and the walls allows for the housing of machinery, bracket fittings, lights and other functional components. The aluminium is a perfect match for the different formal solutions; laminates, beams and castings.

The second phase of the architectural work concerned the specific projects contained within the overall intervention. Access to the inter-

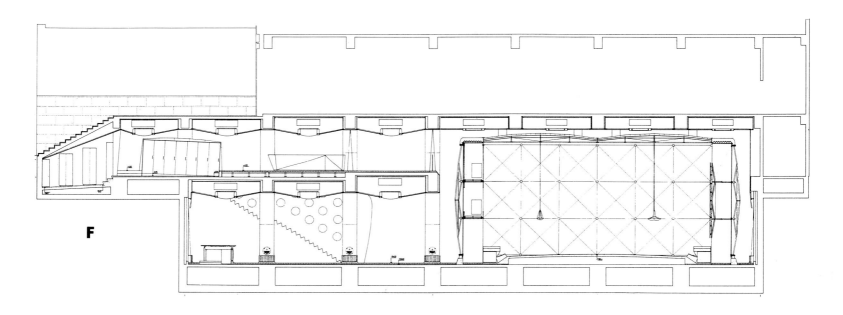

F

Lengthways section of the elevation of the basement and mezzanine. (F)

ior is either through the main doorway in the facade or through a passage which leads to the surrounding streets. From a lobby situated in this corridor access can be gained to The Waiting Bar and The VIP Bar. The washrooms are located on both sides of the stairway with the bars on either side of this floor which has been designed as a meeting area.

At the entrance to the passage there is a metallic footbridge leading onto a spiral staircase which goes down to the ground floor where the great transparent glass box housing the dance floor is located with its sophisticated system of laser illumination, motorised mirrors and delayed sound. Access to the dance area is through four automatic doors which allow for the required volume to be maintained within the box and protect the rest of the space from an excess of sound. The glass box struc-

View from behind one of the bar areas in the basement. (B3)

Partial view of The Vitamin Bar. (C3)

On the following page, one of the bar areas in the basement,
with a view of the discotheque through the glass box which
holds it. (B5, C1)

Above, perspective of the basement access stairs. (B2, D2)

On the left, detail sketches of the restaurant. (B4, D3)

On the left, detail sketches of the entrances to the discotheque. (B6, C4)

Below, one of the entrances doors to the great glass box which holds the dance area. (B)

ture converts the dance area into both a show piece and a view point and as a result all of the different atmospheres are visually combined enhancing the idea of total space.

Three bar counters in the form of tongues are located in the basement: at the back there is a counter serving fast food, which can be eaten at folding tables found alongside. Between the bars two access stairways lead up to the restaurant which consists of three hanging platforms and enjoys a privileged view of the rest of the space. Long ramps lead to The Ice Bar and The Vitamin Bar. The first appears to be a hermetic structure in the style of a large fridge, where chilled liqueurs from all over the world are served. The second has a sinuously shaped bar counter where drinks are mixed containing a variety of vitamins, a result of the Japanese fashion for the daily consumption of physical and mental stimulants.

The finishing touches to the overall image of the premises are provided by the design of the decorations, furnishings, graphics, wardrobe, signs, etc., with every conceivable detail being taken into account and used in either harmonious or contrasted combinations in order to create an implicitly recreational universe.

All of these aspects have contributed to the creation of an autonomous and independent universe where a new concept of leisure has been formulated. The intention of the creative team that worked on this project was the realisation of a different kind of space where architecture and the creative arts would be moulded together in the materialisation of an integrated form of entertainment, implicit in the concept of crossing, and organised within a new dimension of recreational space where it is possible to eat, drink, dance or chat in an atmosphere that is both innovative and highly creative.

Above, partial view of the dance floor of the discotheque. (B5, C4)

A view of one of the communication galleries between the different levels of the premises. (C5)

Detail of one of the entrances to the discotheque. (B)

Below, detail sketches of the decoration of the premises and perspective of the main staircase from the ground floor. (A4)

IL PALLAZZO BARS

Gaetano Pesce, Ettore Sottsass, Shiro Kuramata y Aldo Rossi

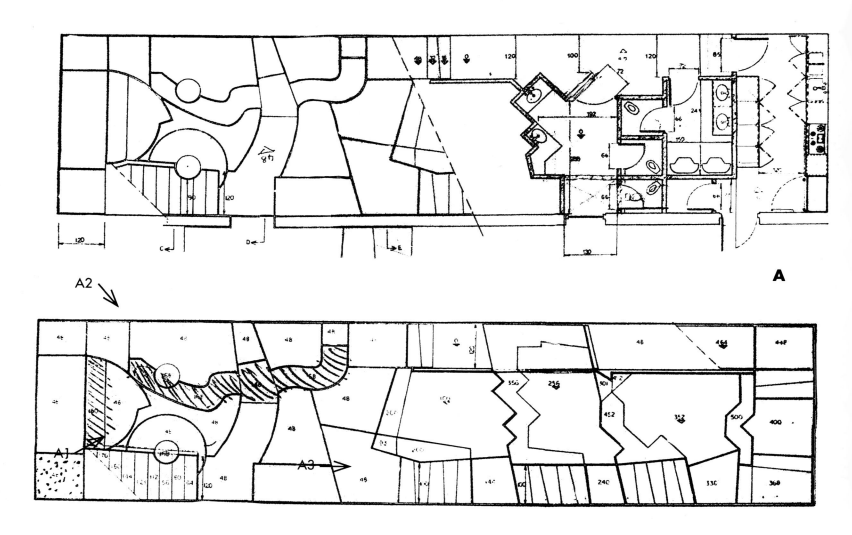

Floor plans for the Listón Bar, the work of Gaetano Pesce, an authentic example of colouring combining angular and other more voluptuous forms. The space is distributed at different levels and connected by a system of stairways running through the interior, without the perception of the unity whole ever being lost. (A)

On the following page, a view of the different levels of the premises, on one of which a peculiar oxidised steel music booth can be seen. (A3)

View of the Listón from another angle, featuring an original design for furnishings and the pattern of the floors. (A1)

Panoramic view of the sinuous form of the bar counter. A series of small fixed spots are the basis of the lighting of the bar which, together with the decoration, contributes to the creation of an electric atmosphere. (A2)

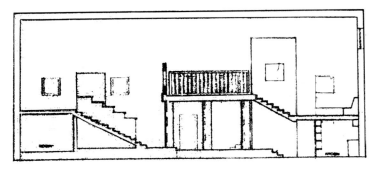

SECTION A-A'

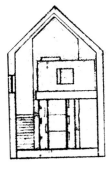 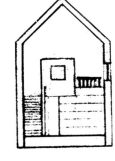

SECTION C-C'   **SECTION D-D'**

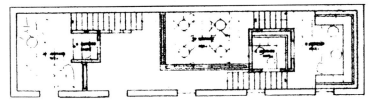

UPPER LEVELS PLAN

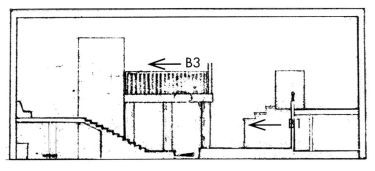

B3

SECTION B-B'

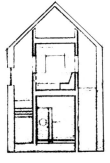   **B**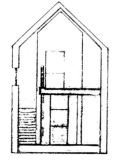

SECTION E-E'   **SECTION F-F'**

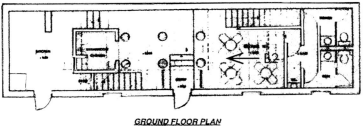

GROUND FLOOR PLAN

Within the Il Palazzo Hotel complex and situated in the two modules that run parallel to the central building there are four premises which serve as bar-restaurants, each of them designed by one of the great internationally recognised names, one of which is the architect for the hotel project, Aldo Rossi. These four bars, all open to the public, are the Listón by Gaetano Pesce, the Zibibbo by Ettore Sotsass, the Obslomova by Shiro Kuramata, and the El Dorado which is the work of Rossi.

In each of the premises a totally different atmosphere is created: the Listón is an authentic sensory explosion of voluptuous forms and florid colours, with a structural lay-out on different levels.

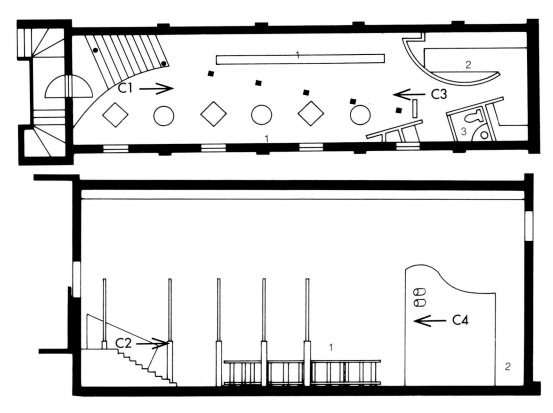

Floor plans and elevation of the Obslomova by Shiro Kuramata. (C)

On the previous page, overall view of the bar, an intimate interior design, achieved through the use of soft and warm tones, the lightness of the glass furnishings and the artificial illumination successfully creating a cosy atmosphere. (C1, C2). Below, a perspective of the bar from the opposite angle to the previous photo, with the great wooden stairway in the background. (C3, C4)

In the Zibibbo by Ettore Sotsass, designed in collaboration with Marco Zanini and Mike Ryan, a Mediterranean atmosphere is recreated where the colours, blue and yellow, evoke the beaches and the sky of the Mare Nostrum.

Shiro Kuramata's Obslomova is a bar with an intimate atmosphere, decorated in soft colours with predominantly light forms both in terms of the furnishings and also in the structure of the space itself.

Finally El Dorado, by Aldo Rossi with the assistance of Morris Adjmi, includes in its design and interior decoration numerous elements characteristic of the decorative language of the hotel with references to the main façade, and the materials used in the furnishings.

In summary four designer bars for the authentically international project of the Il Palazzo Hotel, endorsed by the creativity of four of the world's foremost architectural designers.

On this page and the following, different views of the El Dorado bar by Aldo Rossi and Morris Adjmi. This space, with its angular roof, contains numerous components which form part of the aesthetic language of the hotel, above all the golden reproduction of the illuminated main façade.

HOTELS

HOTEL IL PALAZZO

Aldo Rossi & Shigeru Uchida

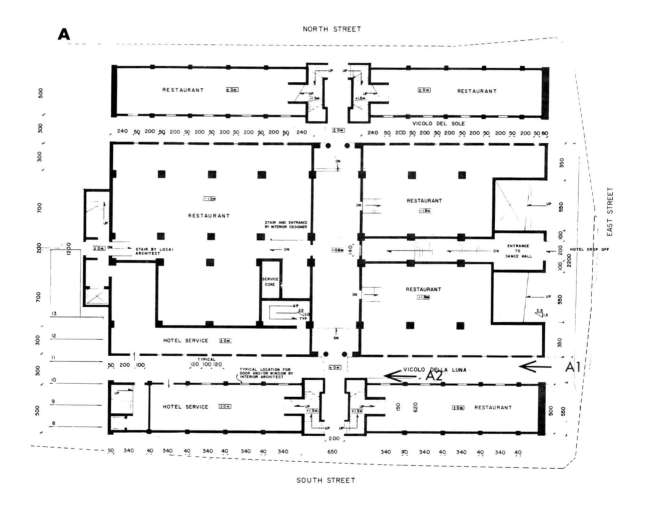

Floor plan of the lower level of the hotel where the different facilities open to the public are located. (A)

At the end of 1986 Mitsushiro Kuzawa, the hotel owner, proposed to Aldo Rossi and Shigeru Uchida the architectural work and the artistic direction for the Il Palazzo Hotel. He also sought the collaboration of an outstanding group of creative designers to work on specific aspects of the project. The objective was to effect a perceptive metamorphosis which would lead to an accomplished social, cultural and intellectual rationale that went further than the merely functional aspect. The design would have to make an impression on the urban landscape of the city (Fukuoka, in Japan) through the force of its visual impact, thus converting the building into the reorganisational centre of a cityscape which was marked out by an imoderate diversity. Many

A view of the main façade, a structure based on the symmetrical disposition of vertical columns and horizontal cornices in copper, the soft green hues contrasting with the reddish tones of the stonework. The overall layout is shown with the plaza as the articulating axis and the platform as the base. (B1, C1)

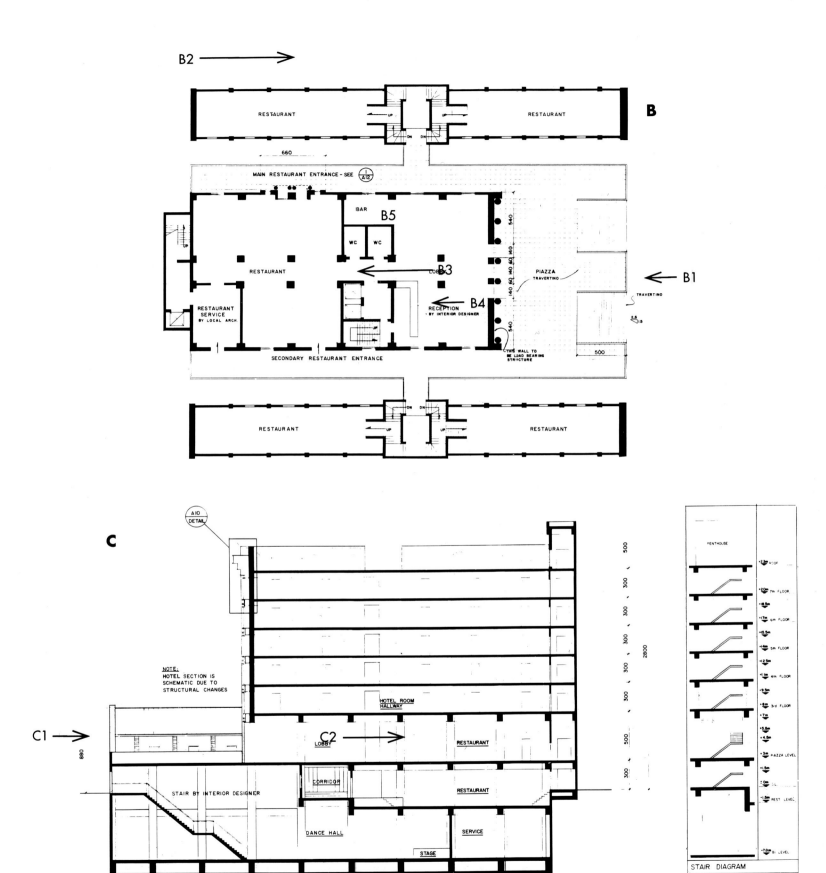

B2 →

B

RESTAURANT   RESTAURANT

UP   DN   DN   UP

660

MAIN RESTAURANT ENTRANCE - SEE ①/A12

BAR

B5

WC   WC

RESTAURANT   LOBBY **B3** ←

540
140 80 80 140
140 80 80 140
540

PIAZZA
TRAVERTINO

← **B1**

TRAVERTINO

UP

RESTAURANT
SERVICE
BY LOCAL ARCH

RECEPTION ← **B4**
BY INTERIOR DESIGNER

THIS WALL TO
BE LOAD BEARING
STRUCTURE

500

SECONDARY RESTAURANT ENTRANCE

RESTAURANT   RESTAURANT

DN   DN
UP   UP

C

A10
DETAIL

NOTE:
HOTEL SECTION IS
SCHEMATIC DUE TO
STRUCTURAL CHANGES

500

300

300

300

300

300

2800

HOTEL ROOM
HALLWAY

C1 →

880

C2 →
LOBBY   RESTAURANT

500

STAIR BY INTERIOR DESIGNER

CORRIDOR

RESTAURANT

300

DANCE HALL

SERVICE

STAGE

PENTHOUSE

ROOF
7th FLOOR
6th FLOOR
5th FLOOR
4th FLOOR
3rd FLOOR

PIAZZA LEVEL

REST LEVEL

B LEVEL

STAIR DIAGRAM

On the previous page, above, floor plan of the ground floor of the hotel (B) and, below, elevation section of the central block. (C)

A view of one of the side façades of the hotel. (B2)

On the left different perspectives of Moon Street illustrating the tile work and the lighting, and in the photo below, the entrance to the Obslomova bar. (A1, A2)

of the fundamental characteristics resulting from the design are based on these objectives: consistency, opacity, an image of immutable serenity, yet the building also emanates a timeless air which will guarantee the durability of this work over and beyond the vicissitudes of fashionable currents and trends.

Aldo Rossi and Shigeru Uchida, the principal architect and the artistic director, have shown themselves to be two of the great names in the field of architecture and interior design for many years. For the design of the interior of this project they worked with a creative group of the highest quality.

Aldo Rossi after many years of combining an intense educational and professional activity became internationally recognised through the award of the first prizes in the Carlo Felice Theatre Competition in Genoa in 1984, The German History Museum Prize in Berlin (1988), and the Pritzker Architecture Prize in 1989. Outstanding examples of his work include the Palace of Congresses in Milan, the Casa Aurora in Turin and the Arco de Galveston and the Centro Torri in Parma. Rossi's creative trajectory has been associated with the construction of buildings which attempt to influence both the collective memory and the urban environment. His work is a further example of that European tradition of the monument conceived as a timeless witness to the human condition and, at the same time, as a definition of the contemporary cityscape.

The Japanese designer, Shigeru Uchida, has for many years been noted for the outstanding variety of his work which was recognised in 1987 with his obtaining the prestig-

On this page and the following, overall view of the complex, showing the details of the structure designed by Aldo Rossi with the plaza as the articulating axis, the base platform for the main building, the lateral annexes and the entrance to the lower level where the leisure multi-space Barna Crossing is situated. The location of the hotel itself can also be observed, in its role as a key visual axis in the multiform urban environment of the city of Fukoaka.

ious Mainichi Design Award. His collection of chairs, September 1977, features in the permanent exhibition of the Metropolitan Museum of Modern Art, in New York. Uchida's most representative projects are the Roppongi Wave Building (Tokyo, 1983); the Japanese Government Pavilion for the Tsukuba Expo '85; Le Club bar; the Yuzutei restaurant (1986); and the Ginza Micaldy shop (1990) in Tokyo. His exhibitions in New York, Belgium, Paris and Tokyo and the publication of various specialist books attest to the cultural significance of this creative designer.

The name given to this project is an indica-

A elevation of the façade of the hotel. (D)

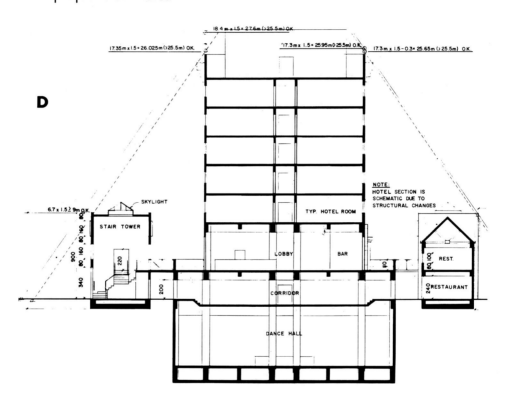

tion of the intentions of architect and designer; palazzo conjures up a style of life which combines luxury, art and intellectuality, within a typically European conceptual line of thought, which is here adapted to the functional demands of the hotel.

The techniques employed to make an impact on the urban landscape were based on the use of an essentially European architectural language where the component of the plaza takes on a predominant role of formal

and structural distribution, here conceived in the form of a platform upon which the main building was located. The space was divided on the basis of a constructive strategy of classical-renaissance reminiscences, which were adapted to the differentiation of levels. The upper level takes in the first eight floors, and the lower level, in the shape of a prism with a horizontal tendency, includes the ground floor and the basement and serves as the base for the hotel. On this lower level there are various

Different views of the side exits of the hotel through the annexes.

On the previous page, perspective of the corridor which runs across the length of the ground floor of the hotel from the reception to the restaurant, the entrance to which can be seen in the background. The four sided columns and circular capital in granite distribute the space organising the layout of the different areas. (B3, C2)

Different views of the decoration of the hotel lobby.

In the central photo, an overall view of the reception with its regular organisation of materials and tonalities, illustrated by the contrast between the Chinese quince wood with its red and brown shades, and the unusual granite with its onyx pigmentation and characteristic greenish colour. (B4)

In the detail photos on this page and the following, different views of the bar on the ground floor of the hotel which exhibits the same aesthetic characteristics as the reception area. (B5)

facilities open to the public, principally the recreational complex Barna Crossing. Italian style stairways flank the entrance to the subterranean area and ascend to the two modules which run parallel to the lateral façades of the hotel where four bars open to the public are located: the Russian style space of Shuru Kuramata's Obslomova; Gaetano Pesce's

the parallel areas across metallic footbridges, suspended from structures in the form of towers, overlooked by a circular clock. To the west and at the back there is a car park.

The emblematic strength of the work rests in the front elevation of the façade, suggesting an image of serenity and grandeur, an elegant combination of western classicism and eastern

Listón; the Zibibbo by Ettore Sottsass; and El Dorado by Rossi himself.

Two interior passages separate the platform from these modules: to the north Sun Street, and to the south Moon Street. The fine tile work and the lighting strategy make these small passages ideal for relaxing or taking a stroll. From the plaza access can be gained to

formalism. Iranian stone of a reddish hue which varies according to the light and the atmospheric conditions was used in the construction.

Those spaces characteristic of a hotel appear in the main body of the building conceptually and formally related to the nature of the exterior area. The main lobby was divided

into a reception area on the right and a large bar with a waiting area. In the reception area the interplay of pillars and the furnishings contribute to the creation of a warm and welcoming atmosphere which is enhanced by the covering on the walls and the ceiling. Access to the restaurant is gained through a simple marble entrance way. The criteria for the dis-

tribution, decoration and gastronomic choice of the restaurant are a synthesis of Japanese and Italian tendencies. The design of the bedrooms was the work of Ikuyo Mitsuhashi who maintained the style of cultural fusion with both western and eastern accessories. The 62 bedrooms were fitted out with furniture designed specifically for the hotel perfectly combining aesthetics with functionality.

Overall perspective of the hotel reception. (B4)

On the previous page, detail of the bar counter and the design of the chairs in the ground floor bar. (B5)

In this first Japanese experience Aldo Rossi, with the assistance of Shigeru Uchida, managed to cross the cultural frontier and to adapt his construction methods to the functional and aesthetic demands of the country, achieving a singularly natural fusion of the creative universes of the West and the East in this palazzo in the heart of Japan.

View of one of the passages on the upper floors of the hotel.

On the right and below, different views of the decoration of the rooms which are designed in a western style, except those of the seventh floor decorated by Kyo-Juaku in an oriental style with the typical tatami and Japanese cedar wood and rice paper as basic materials.

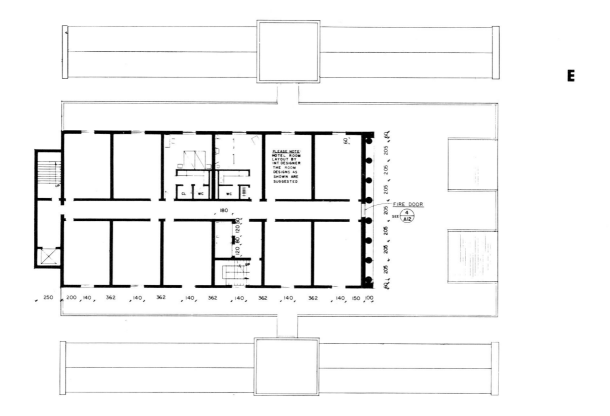

E

A view of one of the western style bedrooms.

THE SHERATON HOTEL

Platou Arkitekter A/S

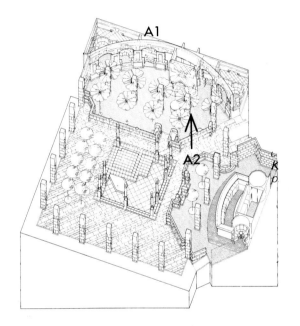

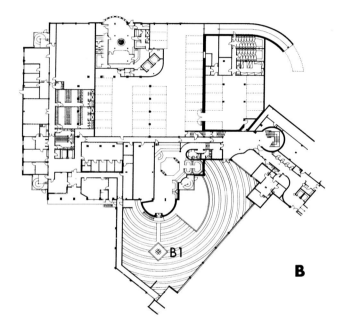

Floor plan of the ground floor of the Sheraton Hotel, the atrium and adjacent area. (A)

Floor plan of one of the upper floors. (B)

Plans of one of the hotel's restaurants, the Orchidée with the entrance in the central atrium. (C)

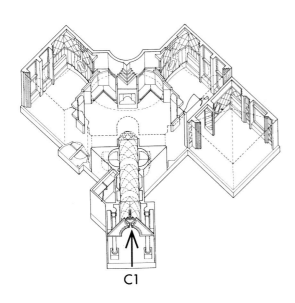

C1

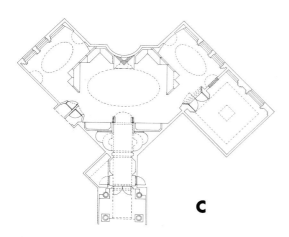

C

During the eighties the owners of a disused factory in Oslo, decided to rebuild and convert it into a convention centre and hotel. The Sheraton Hotel Company took over the hotel, making it part of their worldwide chain and Platou Arkitekter A/S, one of the leading interior design companies in Norway, took the project on.

Platou Arkitekter has worked on projects for financial institutions, businesses and governments throughout the world, and have also been involved in an extensive range of work including architectural and interior design, urban planning, and even ship design. The projects are carried out by a group of ninety architects and designers under the direction of the six principal partners.

The main problem with the Sheraton Hotel project, according to the architects themselves, lay in the unattractiveness of the area in which the building stood, surrounded by constructions on a monumental scale: a motorway raised 12 metres above ground level, the convention centre approximately 40 metres in width and 90 metres in length, and the Kjorbo Heights building which stands 40 metres. This environment made it necessary that the hotel should be concieved with definitive forms that would be in proportion to its environment and would result in a somewhat cold exterior. To counter this the architects sought an interior design of great warmth and intimacy which would extend a friendly and welcoming atmosphere to guests and visitors.

In the words of the architects, «The element of surprise is fundamental. From the moment in which you enter the hotel there is a theatrical image of grandeur which is the cornerstone of the conception of the architectural style. As soon as you cross the threshold of the atrium there is an immediate isolation from the outside world». The atrium links the main areas of the hotel, the reception, the bar, the restaurants and the convention hall all of encompassed by a gallery. The centre of

the atrium features a figure framed by columns, erected around a sculpture by the Norwegian artist Knut Steen.

The 260 rooms occupy four of the six floors of the hotel, the rooms and the passages which separate them are built in such a way that they serve as bridging-pieces between the exterior façade and the twenty columns erected in the atrium.

On the left, perspective of a passage in one of the service areas. (D1) Below, floor plan of one of the hotel's restaurants. (D)

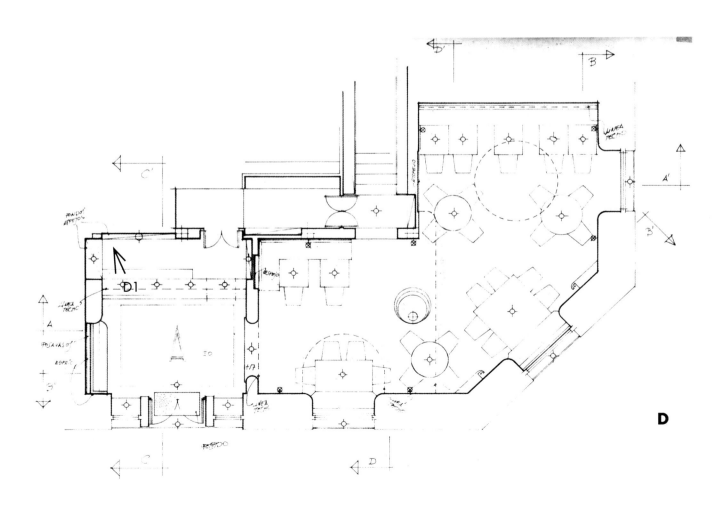

D

Lighting is one of the bases of the interior design of the hotel emphasising to a great degree the theatricality of the design. A sophisticated system of computers controls a range of luminescent scenes which change gradually throughout the day.

Aesthetically one of the architects' ideas was to convert the central atrium in such a way that the central area of the building with its cobble-stoned flooring would symbolise the street, while at night the rooms would complement this imaginary urban landscape, adding a variable and theatrical lighting pattern to a scene reminiscent of a cityscape.

The material forms and colours used in the interior of the hotel bear absolutely no relation to those used on the outside, emphasising the contrast between the coldness of the external environment and the interior warmth which was the authentic leitmotif of the project.

The initial aim of focusing attention on the interior, given the unattractiveness of the surrounding landscape and the exterior of the hotel itself was fully achieved. The warm and welcoming sensation that the guest or visitor is intended to encounter was ensured by means of an interior design which skilfully combined the distribution of space, the decorative materials employed and above all the original lighting system which creates distinct yet uniformly warm atmospheres.

Panoramic view of the atrium roof showing the computer controlled play of lighting effects and the lay-out of some of the rooms around the central space. (A1), (B1)

On the previous page, above, space covered by the atrium, with the marble columns and the sculpture by Knut Steen in the centre (A2). Below, the entrance to one of the hotel's restaurants (C1).

On this page, elevators at the main entrance to the hotel.

HOTEL LA VILLA

Marie-Christine Dorner

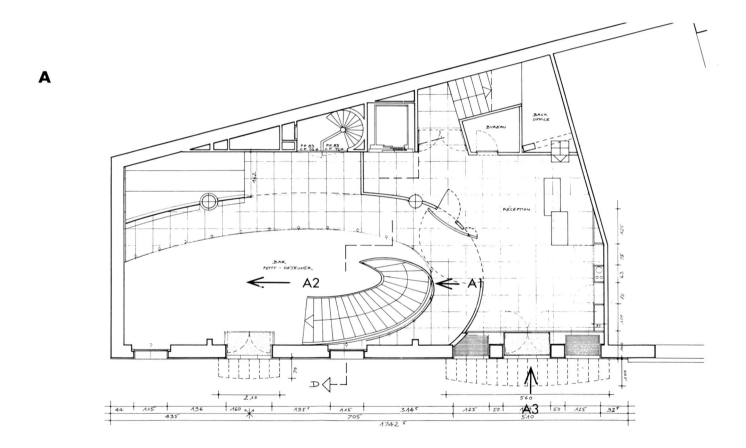

Floor plan of the ground floor of the Hotel La Villa, including the reception, the communicating stairways and the bar on the level above.

On the following page, overall view of the bar and its access stairway. (A1)

On the left, another view of the hotel bar. (A2)

Detail of the Hotel La Villa logo.

The Hotel La Villa is a small four star estab-lishment of 35 rooms situated in Saint Germaine des Prés in Paris. The young French designer Marie-Christine Dorner planned and carried out the complete renovation of the old hotel, which in turn had been based on the reconversion of an old mansion previously occupying the site.

Born in Strasbourg in 1960, Dorner set off to travel the world after graduating from the Ecole Camondo arriving in Japan in 1986. It was there that she designed her first projects, which included a furniture collection and the interior decoration for a clothes shop in Tokyo. She set up her own pratice in Paris in 1987 and since that time has worked with companies such as Cassina, Baccarat and Scarabat who have produced her designs for porcelain, coffee tables, chairs and arm-chairs. Her work has been presented in vari-ous prestigious exhibitions, including Design François 1960-1990 at the George Pompidou Centre and Avant Première in London.

The reception area is located on the ground floor, on the left the great curved stair-case which winds up from the basement to the bar which is located on an upper level look-ing down on the entrance. The walls are clad with violet coloured leather, recalling the colour of the carpet, and the floor and some of the walls are faced with a blue coloured stone.

In the basement there is a bar with music which has a separate entrance from the street, as does the saloon bar on the level above the ground floor.

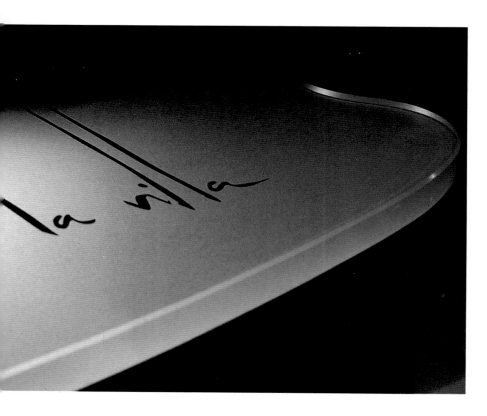

Above, right, a view of the entrance to the hotel. On the rest of the page, different details of the decoration and the furniture including the detail of the room numbers projected onto the floor.

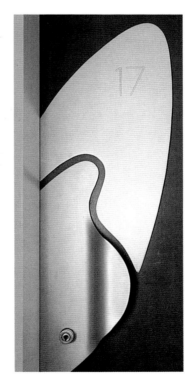

Perspective of one of the rooms, in this case with agreen
predominance, illustrating a fundamentally practical type
of decoration which loses sight of aesthetic values.

The rooms, although maintaining a certain conformity, are individually distinct in terms of shape and colour. The entrance to each room, the wardrobe and the bathroom are finished in materials such as marble, glass, mirrored surfaces and nickel with the ceiling at a uniform height framing a homogenous space which although cold remains comfortable. The ceilings are covered in taffeta either in blue, chestnut, copper, honey, almond, ochre, orange, red or green tones, a different colour for each room. The vertical surfaces are of a much more sober appearance, painted in lighter hues.

The lighting installation is innovative, in that the main lights can be easily regulated. There is the useful addition of a permanent night-light in the bathrooms.

The corridors are transitory places, darker, more sober and aesthetically neutral. An unusual detail is the projection of the room numbers onto the floor in front of each door.

The Hotel La Villa is the fruit of the creative imagination of its designer and since its remodelling, has become a small and welcoming establishment the originality of which rests in the choice of room colour, depending on the feeling or atmosphere required by each guest.

Overall view of the bathroom of one of the rooms, showing the rich combination of the materials used including marble.

On the right, overall view of one of the bedrooms showing the design of the furniture.

Above and on the right, details of the lighting and the furniture. On the following page, a partial view of one of the washrooms.

SCANDIC CROWN HOTEL

Gert Wingardh & Anders Wilhelmson

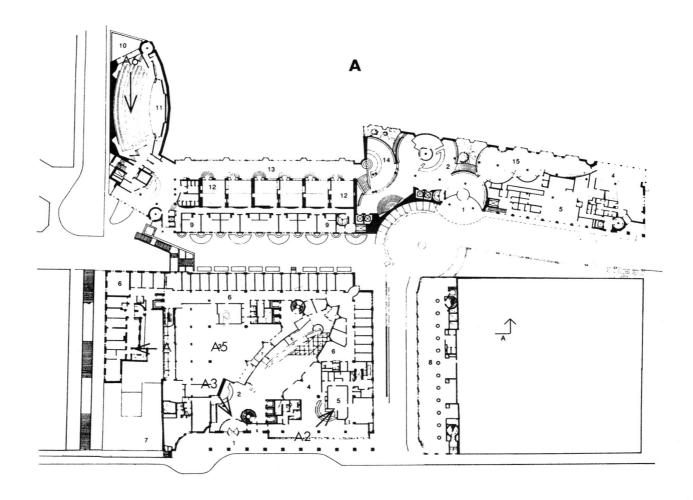

Floor plan of the hotel, showing the location of the three modules. (A)

On the following page, the stairs located in the main building, the distribution of which is based on a juxtaposition of the circular areas in the form of balustrades dominating the whole of the lobby area. (A1, B1)

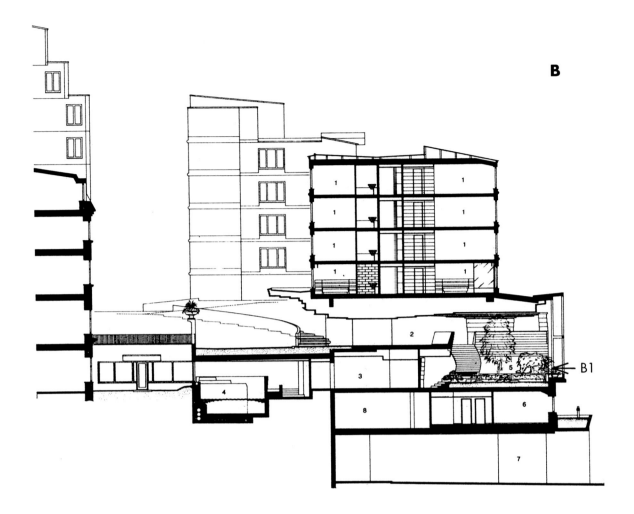

An elevation of the main building. (B)

This Stockholm hotel which was remodelled in 1989, represents an unequivocal statement of the architectural pattern and interior design characteristics of the Nordic countries; a close relationship with the exterior, above all to capture as much natural light as possible, and a rational distribution of the different functional spaces. To these constants the architects have added a concept of interior design based on the juxtaposition of circular surfaces, in which the distinct areas are elegantly distributed outlining a sweep that is logical and effective in its conjunction of the different modules of the hotel and also in the creation of an atmosphere that benefits from a diaphanous luminosity.

In 1985 Gert Wingardh and Anders Wilhelmson began a period of professional collaboration which lasted until 1988, when the company which they had formed broke up,

A view of the hotel bar, located in a semicircular space to the right of the reception area. (A2)

becoming Wingardh & Wingardh AB and Wilhelmson AB Arkitekter Och Designers. Since that time the career of the Wingardh has been principally centred on the design of commercial interiors. At the present time Wingardh is working for the industrial pharmaceutical company Hestra on the construction of laboratory buildings. Wilhelmson for his part has consistently worked in the commercial field designing showrooms and different objects. Among his clients are Vitra International of Switzerland and the Swedish Telecommunications Administration, for whom he has designed a project for a supervision centre. He also lectures at the Stockholm School of Architecture. The hotel consists of three diverse morphological volumes the largest of which is based on an extended rectangular floor. The second presents a similar image but on a different plane, a semicircular structure, forming the front façade which links these two volumes. The last module was in a slightly curved form with a highly dynamic look. The continual changes in the elevation and the intersecting planes, resulting from the adaptation of the building to the terrain, are the principal factors determining the dispersed volume of the hotel.

The architects basing themselves on the above pattern drew up a functional distribution related to the physical characteristics of each body. The main body was to be the entrance and reception area, also including services areas such as the bar and the restaurant. In the second module the conference hall and meeting rooms were located, while the last, due to its partially curved design, housed the auditorium. Two small atriums were built between these three modules linking them on the ground floor level, where recreational areas such as the pool and the sauna were installed. Access to this lower level is gained by two stairways, one of which leads down from the lobby.

In order to achieve an overall uniformity throughout the complex a uniform lighting and decoration structure was employed in all three modules. The material processes, colour scheme and ornamentation determine an interior which is characterised by its dazzling whiteness, apparent in the majority of the structural elements, and the harmonious influ-

Above, view of the lifts to the upper floors of the hotel.

In the photo below, a partial view of the restaurant characterised by the disconnected disposition of the planes of various curved wall facings, featuring a variety of scope and direction. (A5)

Perspective of the auditorium in the third module of the hotel. (A6)

View of the lifts in the main building with one of the balustrades characteristic of the first module of the hotel.

ence of the natural light which floods in from
the exterior. Materials of an essentially cold
character such as white marble and grey
granite were used for the flooring, the design
concept was based on the treatment of different types of wood (cherry, birch, pear),
enhancing the creation of a warm and welcoming atmosphere, which is characteristic of

Another view of the restaurant and the access stairway to
the upper level. (A5)

Partial view of the underground pool framed by two of the wall facings; one of wooden panels and the other slightly curved and covered in tiles.

Below, a view of one of the washrooms with marble as the principal material. A set of three mirrors gives the interior a spacious and transparent feeling.

the complex as a whole.

The design of the Scandic Crown Hotel is a fine example of those schemes which are most representative of Nordic architecture and design, applied in this case to a distribution conditioned by a volumetric inequality and the particularity of the location of the modules.

Another perspective of the pool showing one of the walls facings, consisting of wooden panels with small square openings which filter the exterior light.

RESTAURANTS

BEDDINGTON'S RESTAURANT

Borek Sipek

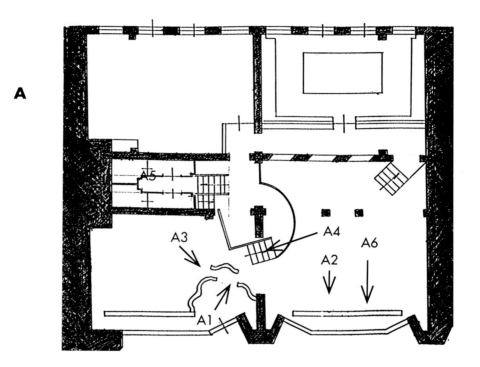

The original restaurant, owned by Jeanny Beddington, and located on the ground floor of a building in Amsterdam was architecturally conceived by Koen van Velsen in 1986. Due to its structural and aesthetic characteristics, which were apparently out of tune with the taste of the targeted clientele, the need for a programme of transformation in terms of the image of the premises was evident. Due to restrictions of time and money the scale of the work was limited to a remodelling of the façade, the entrance and the washrooms on the basis of which a redefinition of the style of the restaurant had to be achieved.

The project, completed in 1989, was entrusted to the Czech architect Borek Sipek who became professionally established in 1983 after many years of work as professor of the theory of design at the University of Essen. He has worked for design companies as important as Driada, Flos and Sawaya & Moroni in Italy; Quartett in Germany; Neotu, Sèvre and Daum in France; Leitner and Wittman in Austria; and Alterego and Artifort in Holland. His work has been awarded numerous prizes and exhibited in the most prestigious artistic venues around the world. His distinguished mention in the 1983 edition of the German Architectural Prize, awarded for his glass house in Hamburg, and the Kho Liang design prize in 1988 are worthy of note.

Floor plan of the premises.

The owner of the premises proposed, to Sipek, that a significant transformation of the interior and the exterior of the restaurant, including the renovation and redecoration of the washrooms, should be attempted without any construction work being done.

In order to achieve this Sipek had to resolve the spatial conflicts deriving from the original

Panoramic view of the two walls situated at the entrance to the restaurant, showing the separation between Sipek's intermediate wall and the original glazed façade. (A1)

111

On the right, a view of the separating wall with openings characteristic of the architect's own aesthetic language through which natural light filters. (A2). Below, overall view of the structures located inside the entrance. (A3)

On the following page, different views of Sipek's two principal interventions the two walls at the entrance and the location of an intermediate wall between the restaurant and the glazed façade. (A4)

structure and distribution. The principal problem was the glazed frontal façade which, due to the reduced dimensions of the premises, converted the privacy of eating and drinking into activities performed in a shop window openly visible to the passers by. A solution had to be found in order to preserve the intimacy of the clients yet without renouncing the advantages offered by the natural light. To this end an intermediate wall was erected between the diners and the façade which acted as a protective screen and as an interior façade for the restaurant. The introduction of this visual delimiter protected the privacy of the diners through the establishment of a physical barrier, the facings of which were located just a few centimetres from the glazed façade and considerably altered the view of the premises from the street.

The plastic characteristics of the wall derives from its colour scheme and the openings in the form of rectangular windows of different sizes. The warmth of the yellow and ochre tones used in the colour scheme is in marked contrast to the coldness of the architecture and the whiteness of the structural elements. The light source was rendered more diffuse enhancing the creation of an intimate and welcoming atmosphere.

Another aspect of Sipek's intervention is the disposition in the entrance of three sinuous structures dramatising the moment of entry through the use of voluptuous lines and a biomorphic style, elements which are close to the heart of the architect. The yellow colouring is brought back here, but with much more intensity emphasising the junction of the curved planes and contrasting with the subdued nature of the overall colour scheme.

The last area affected by the change was the washrooms for which a platform was designed with access stairs and a decoration based on the use of tiles.

Insofar as functional criteria are concerned, the pattern of distribution and the original organisation were maintained, as were the furnishings and the flooring, Sipek's work having been specifically limited to a transformation of the visual perception of the restaurant.

The project was designed with brilliance thanks to the consummate skill with which Sipek, through the remodelling of three elements, conjured up a total transformation of the atmosphere of the restaurant through a perfectly measured use of the most significant elements of his own distinctive creative language.

On the previous page, a view of one of the washrooms and detail of the same. (A5)

A panoramic view of the restaurant area, with the separating wall in the background, in the upper part of which are a series of small windows which softly diffuse the natural light. In the lower part of the wall the openings are larger and are covered by light drapes of soft white and yellow fabrics. (A6)

Below, a perspective of the premises, with the platform and the stairs which lead to the washrooms partially visible to the left of the photo.

L' HORT DE LES MONGES

Alfredo Arribas

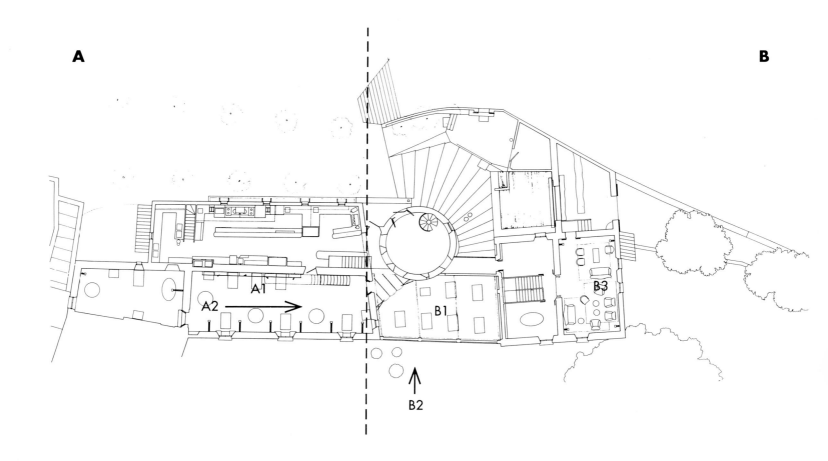

Floor plan of the main building and adjacent areas.

On the right, a night view of the main building.

The initial objective of this project was the extension and refurbishing of the L'Hort de les Monges restaurant, a large rambling premises surrounded by old abandoned and run down outbuildings. The stairways, walkways, terraces, dining rooms, patios and gardens are freely distributed around the area, constituting a space of almost labyrinthine qualities. The first problem was the restoration and rebuilding of the ruined parts of the restaurant, after which the whole had to be given a new equilibrium, a certain aesthetic and functional unity.

The Barcelona architect Alfredo Arribas brought his skill and experience to bear on this project basing the transformation on the construction of a circular tower, which became the nexus for the union of the different unconnect-

An exterior view of part of the façade and of the circular tower. (B2)

117

A view of the portico on the second floor. Above, detail sketch of the portico arch seen from the restaurant and, below, part of the restaurant.

Above, a partial view of the restaurant and the arch which gives onto the portico on the floor above. (A1)

On the left, entrance reception area, and below, the passages and corridors of the stairway which runs round the building.

ed bodies; the barns, the stables and later additions. The tower was built in the traditional Catalan style and includes a wine cellar, the reception area and the offices.

The difference in level between the two lengthways façades is dealt with by means of a stoop which runs round the building. The restaurant is located on the ground floor of the Masia farm house itself and the bar occupies the smallest of the existing outbuildings with an adjacent terrace. Generally speaking the different spaces have been restored with few modifications, the expression of a sincere respect for the traditional architecture of the original buildings.

The materials for this extension and refurbishment were used in their natural state and

A view of the bar counter.

traditional almost forgotten craft methods, such as rough stone work, lime casting, the use of oxidised iron, undressed timbers and Catalan style vaults, were employed. The use of traditional building methods contributed to the creation of a highly suggestive contrast between the new elements and the old.

The predominance of natural earth and ochre colours was fundamental to the creation of a cosy and homely atmosphere which extends an open invitation to enjoy the place and its hospitality, the landscape and the excellent cuisine. The terraces and conservatories, strategically distributed throughout the area, make L'Hort de les Monges much more than just a restaurant, it is also an ideal place to relax and, for a few hours at least, to escape from the frantic pace of city life.

Above, a view of the lounge. (B3)

Interior view of the terrace with it's wattle roof. (B1)

Below, a view of the main dining room, illustrating the predominance of natural colours, such as ochre. (A2)

KABUTO

Iavicoli & Rossi

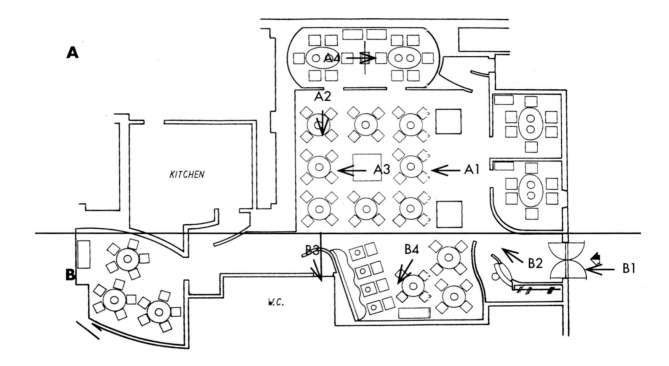

Floor plan of the premises divided into sections.

On the following page, a view of the main dining room illustrating the different decorative elements: the undulating reliefs on the walls, the cobalt blue band which runs round the perimeter, the colour scheme employed as a symbolic reference evocative of a Mediterranean atmosphere and the illumination based on spotlights which emphasise specific points of the room. (A1)

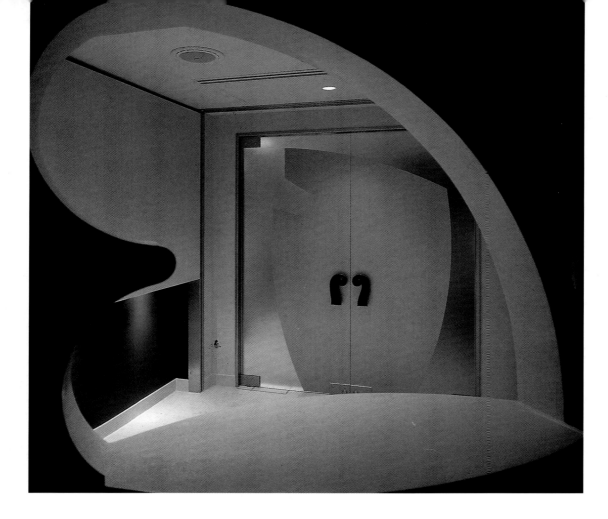

A view of the entrance door to the restaurant. (B1)

Over the last few years Japan has become a rich field for the experimentation of many European designers who find they are are able to develop their creativity in the Japanese market without the constraints which are placed upon them in Europe. Intense competitivity obliges Japanese promoters to seek out and use conceptual and aesthetic originality as a weapon of survival, while the young European architects and designers are attracted by the possibilities of working in a country where intercultural dialogue favours the genesis of suggestive and creative trends.

Vincenzo Iavicoli and Maria Luisa Rossi, two of these young designers, are both Industrial design graduates from the State Institute in Florence. They have been working together since 1980 and in 1985 won the Mainichi Industrial Design Competition in Tokyo for their project for a table-top personal micro-computer. Since 1987 they have been involved in lecturing activities in various universities (Florence, Tsukuba, Tokyo and Montreux) but have continued to work as designers. In 1989 and 1990 they were both living in Japan where they worked on many of the industrial and interior design projects which were to establish their international reputation. In the field of industrial design, their best work includes: the bottle tops for the Titanic bottle, produced by Anthology Quartett (1986); the objects in the Nissay Life Plaza, produced by the Nippon Life Insurance Co. and the Toyota Motor Corporation showroom in 1990. Their outstanding interior design work includes the Metamorphosi Estudio, in Milan, the Daniel Arnaud company studio, in Paris, the hanging sculpture in the Akita Civic and Cultural Centre and the Vestibolo fashion shop in Fukuoka, both in Japan. The work of these two Italian designers has been recognised by numerous publications, through their many exhibitions, and by the award of various international prizes.

For the Kabuto Restaurant project in the Akasaka Tokyu Hotel in the Japanese capital, the Kirin Brewery Co. Ltd., Japan's largest

124

brewery, put their faith in the talent of Iavicoli and Rossi who had already demonstrated their creativity in the Japanese market, through the design of various original spaces. The concept and the aesthetics of the new premises were based on the kaisen-shabu a variant of the traditional shabu-shabu, a culinary creation new to the Japanese gastronomic market. The element of crosscultural symbiosis was supplied by the Italian designers.

The market introduction of this dish, which is cooked in a vessel in the centre of the table and served with a variety of sauces, was the main inspiration for the design of the dining room and the furniture. The decision was made to synthesise Japanese and Mediterranean culture, the aesthetics typical to Japanese cuisine and elements of western design within the one space.

The decoration, the colours and the forms represented the essence of a latin maritime culture and were combined with motifs inspired by Japanese culinary methods.

The public area of the restaurant is focused on the large central room around which isolat-

Perspective of the reception with its slightly curved walls, leading towards the interior entrance behind which the cloakroom and one of the restaurant's smaller rooms are located. The reception was conceived as an advertisement for the atmosphere of the premises, yet it is also illustrative of the reserve and discretion typical of oriental cultures, both open and at the same time closed, a typically Japanese ambiguity. (B2)

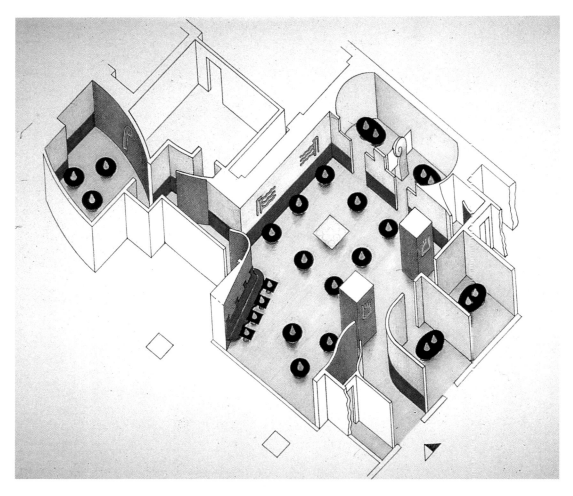

Plan of the distribution of the different rooms.

ed and more intimate spaces were marked off for business lunches and important customers. In this central space the main purpose of the designers was to create a warm and cosy atmosphere within a framework of elegant neutrality: the beige ceiling, the stone used for the flooring and the quartz pigmentation on the walls serve to enhance the spatial unity.

The principal decorative function is reserved for the furniture, particularly the tables, designed by Iavicoli and Rossi, in the form of a counter in the centre of which the vessels, covered by copper lids with a wooden handle, are placed. This element the Kabuto, meaning helmet or headpiece, is the representative symbol of the restaurant. The large tables on which these cooking vessels are kept, when not in use, are also of great aesthetic importance.

The overall effect results from the perfect combination of Mediterranean expressivity in terms of decoration, lighting and symbolic references and innovation in the field of Japanese culinary tradition. The result is a more than noteworthy exercise in intercultural symbiosis resulting from the talent and creativity of the two designers.

A view of one of the sets of table and chairs in the main dining room. (A3)

Design draft for the furnishings of one of the private rooms.

A partial view of the dining room illustrating the design of the chairs in chromed wood and Swedish leather, some with arm rests and high undulating backs. (B3)

A view of the central dining room with the tables which, thanks to the central cooking vessel, serve both for eating and for cooking. (A2)

On the previous page, a view of the oriental screen dividing the space behind the wall, at the back of the central dining room. It can be removed to create a single space. (A4)

A view of the large central table in the main dining room where the vessels used for cooking kaisen-shabu are kept.

Below, a perspective of one area of the restaurant. (B4)

TEATRIZ

Philippe Starck

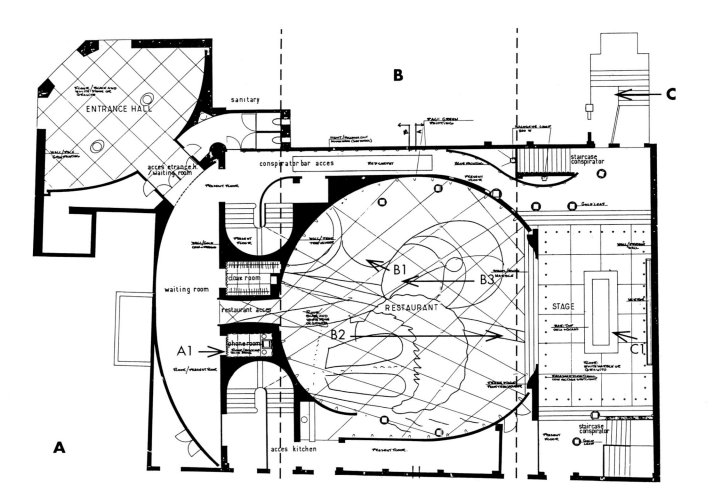

Floor plan and lay-out of Teatriz.

Perspective of the old stalls converted into the restaurant.
On the floor a reproduction of a fresco, by De Chirico, the
division into formal colours constituting a suitable setting
for the furniture which is of an exaggerated kitsch design
with wood as its basic material. The old circle can be seen
in the background, converted into a bar area. (B1, D1)

D

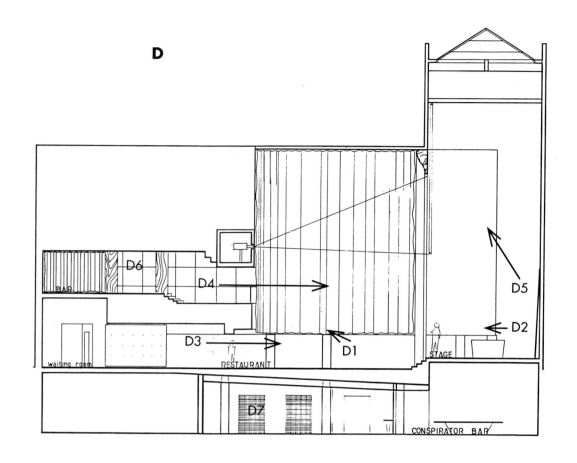

This project was based on an old theatre in Madrid, the remodelling of which was completed in 1990. The objective of the promoters was to create a multi-space for recreational activities, consisting of a bar-restaurant where leisure, music and good food could all be enjoyed in a harmonious setting. The design and interior decoration of the premises were entrusted to

On the previous page, an elevation section of the building, and below, a perspective of the restaurant from the old stage, dominated by the long bar showing the transparent veil and the drapes reflecting the circular structure of the ceiling. (C1, D2)

the architect Philippe Starck who has for many years enjoyed a world wide reputation.

Starck's work, which can be found in the four corners of the globe, has many different facets. In the field of interior design his best work includes: the decoration for the French President's Residence, the Eliseo Palace, in 1984; the Villette, again in Paris and from the same year; the Manin restaurant in Tokyo, in

A view of the restaurant with the stage in the background, illustrating the design of the furnishings; each table has at its head a chair with a stylised back, draped with a cloth which is tied at the side with several bows. Part of the floor with the reproduction of De Chirico's fresco, is also visible. (B2, D3)

1986; and the Royalton (1988) and Paramount (1990) hotels in New York, among many others. Outstanding projects in the field of architecture include: the construction of multi-purpose complexes in Naninani and La Flamme, in 1989; various buildings in Amberes and Osaka (1990); factories, such as SFRI and Laguile and the 18 Kotaro Shimogori residential units in Los Angeles, in 1991. Starck's furniture and Industrial design includes work for important clients throughout the world and has earned him many exhibitions, his work has also been included in the permanent collections of the museums of decorative arts in Paris, London and New York. In 1985 he was named the Creative Designer of the Year and he has received numerous other prizes in recognition of his work.

The Teatriz project presented Starck with the already existing architectural space of an old theatre with a strictly defined lay-out which revealed its previous function. Instead of opting for the complete stripping out of the interior, apparently the easiest solution, Starck decided to use the original distribution, seeing it as another element for the development of the interior design and taking full advantage of its highly scenographic qualities.

The building has three floors and various activity areas. The restaurant is on the level corresponding to the old stalls, while the stage

On this page and the following, a view of part of the restaurant and the stage from the first floor illustrating the scenic character of the premises and the multiple decorative details including the drapes, the transparent veils, the mirrors on the walls and the staircases. (D4)

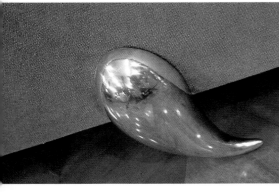

A partial view of the restaurant showing the circle converted into a bar behind the drapes and the access passage in the background (B3, D1). Detail sketches of different decorative elements.

area is now dominated by a long bar. The first floor, previously the dress circle, has been converted into a bar with an area of tables and chairs. The washrooms are in the basement where there is another space where drinks can be taken. The communicating corridors and galleries run round the perimeter of the premises, reflecting the circular form of the building.

The façade was not given any special treatment, the remodelling only becoming apparent once inside the building. Two white columns flank the main entrance framing a reception area with curved ceilings and walls and paved with marble floor tiles laid out in a chess board pattern. The remodelling work is most visible from the area of the old stalls and the stage. The first houses the restaurant and

A view of the area of the old flies of the theatre, where a section of the transparent veil, which envelopes the old stage area, now hangs.

the columns supporting the first floor, and on the site of the original stage there is a bar which has been converted into the visual axis for the different perspectives and the room's principal centre of attention. As well as the structure and the scenographic concept of the old theatre, the curtains and some of the mirrors, used here to amplify certain sequences and perspectives, have also been kept.

A marble staircase descends from below the proscenium to the drinking area which is dominated by a long bar counter and an enormous mirror on the wall which multiplies the play of interior perspectives. The whole space manifests a powerful vertical tendency, reinforced by the use of drapes and by the framing of the stage itself which enhances the theatricality of the original architecture.

Above, a partial view of the stalls converted into a restaurant. (B2, D3)

Different views of the first floor, previously the circle, where there is now a bar. On the right, the small bar and bottle racks, and below, a partial view of the long central bar counter in pink marble with golden wood carvings. (D6)

In what had originally been the circle, there is another bar with tables and chairs which looks down on the restaurant and the central bar counter, finished in pink marble with golden wood carving with drapes once again covering the walls.

A side stairway leads down to the floor below, where another drinking area, and the washrooms are located. The communicating passages were given a cold and geometric treatment which contrasts with the warmer atmosphere of the other spaces.

The Frenchman Philippe Starck has once again demonstrated his dominion over the use of space, distribution and decoration, to create atmospheres, in this case to enhance the theatrical and dramatic spirit of the old building. Teatriz can be considered as an

Another perspective of the long pink marble bar in the circle, with the small golden bar and the bottle racks in the background.

authentic designer's bar, the creative constants of Starck's work come alive in each and every concept, shape and element in an authentic adaptation of the designer's universe to this temple of Madrid nightlife is of an exaggerated kitsch design with wood as its basic material. The old circle can be seen in the background, converted into a bar area

Above, a view of the unusual phone room on the right of the entrance to the restaurant. (A1)

Views of one of the washrooms, decorated in red and gold tones contrasting with the coldness of the white tiles and the halogen lighting. (D7)

Above, a detail sketch of one of the lamps in the transit area.

Views of different corners of the premises.

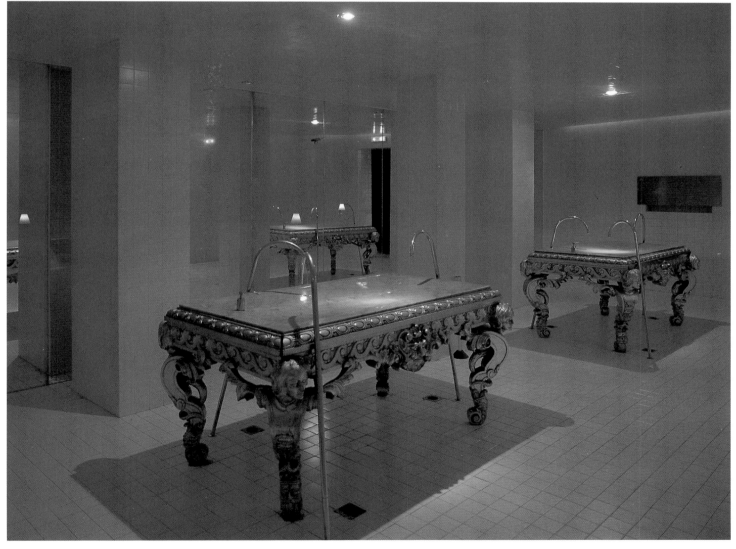

"LE TÉLÉGRAPHE"
RESTAURANT

François-Joseph Graf

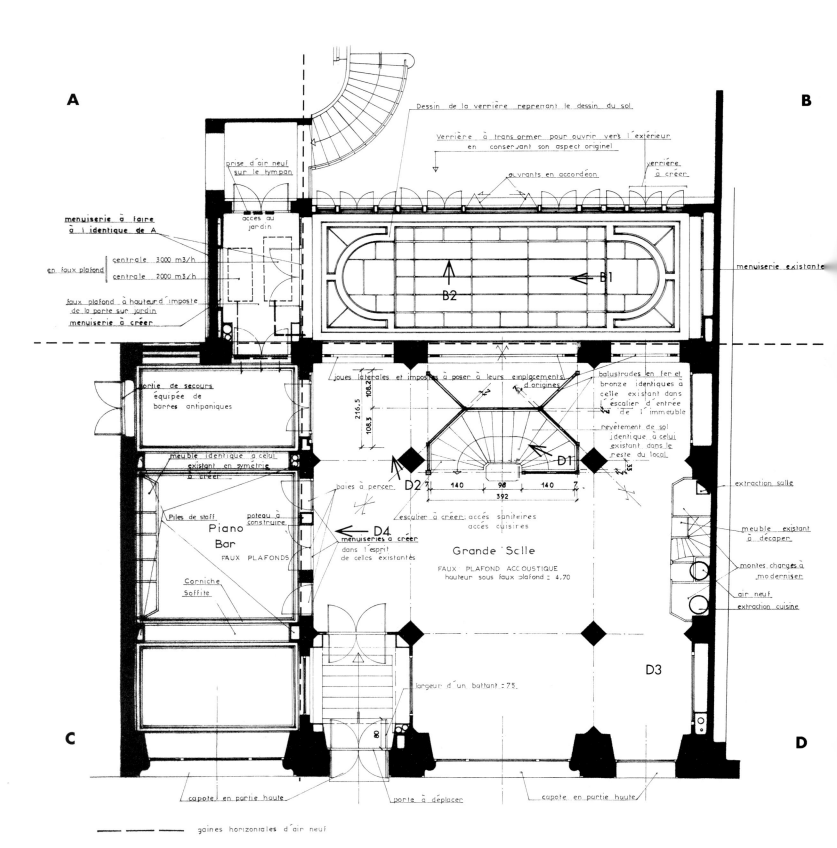

Dessin de la verrière reprenant le dessin du sol

Verrière à transformer pour ouvrir vers l'extérieur en conservant son aspect originel

prise d'air neuf sur le tympan

auvrants en accordéon

verrière à créer

accès au jardin

menuiserie à faire à l'identique de A

menuiserie existante

en faux plafond — centrale 3000 m3/h — centrale 2000 m3/h

faux plafond à hauteur d'imposte de la porte sur jardin
menuiserie à créer

B2

B1

joues latérales et impostes à poser à leurs emplacements d'origines

balustrades en fer et bronze identiques à celle existant dans l'escalier d'entrée de l'immeuble

sortie de secours
équipée de barres antipaniques

revêtement de sol identique à celui existant dans le reste du local

216.5   108.2   108.3

D1

meuble identique à celui existant en symétrie à créer

baies à percer

D2   140   98   140   7
392

extraction salle

Piles de staff

poteau à construire

escalier à créer: accès sanitaires accès cuisines

meuble existant à décaper

Piano Bar
FAUX PLAFONDS

D4   **menuiseries à créer**
dans l'esprit de celles existantes

Grande Salle

montes charges à moderniser

Corniche Soffite

FAUX PLAFOND ACCOUSTIQUE
hauteur sous faux plafond : 4,70

air neuf

extraction cuisine

D3

largeur d'un battant : 75

80

capote en partie haute

porte à déplacer

capote en partie haute

———— gaines horizontales d'air neuf

A view of the glazed gallery. (B1)

Perspective of the balustrade from the stairs which communicate with the main room. (D1)

The building which now houses this restaurant was built in 1907 as an example of social architecture, years later the Maison de Dames des Postes as it was popularly known, was converted into offices, and finally on 12th November 1988 it reopened as a restaurant. The work of conversion, which took several months, was carried out with the greatest respect for the original structure and design and which was authenticated by reference to historical photographs and documents from the beginning of the century.

The architect for this project was the Frenchman François-Joseph Graf, a graduate of the Superior National School of Architecture and Urbanism in Paris who also studied the history of art at the Louvre School. For three years he worked as a collaborator with the chief architect for the Palace of Versailles, and then in 1985 founded the Ariodante studio of architecture and interior design. His most important work includes the L'Ambroisie and Le Télégraphe restaurants and the Antiquarian

On the previous page, floor plan of the premises showing the lay-out.

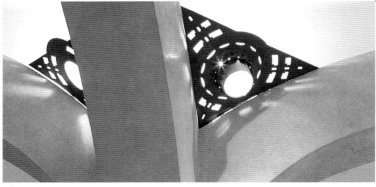

Above, a view of part of the main dining room. (D2)

Detail sketches of the decorated glass partition doors and of one of the spotlights which provide the lighting for the premises. On the following page, a perspective of one of the side areas of the main dining room. (D3)

Biennial, all in Paris. His recent projects have been the Hotel de l'Amirande, in Avignon, and the Club de l'Etoile again in Paris.

Le Télégraphe Restaurant consists of a large room, a piano-bar and a gallery projecting out into the space of the gardens, which, thanks to its glazed structure, provides the restaurant with a marvellous source of natural light. The original height was brought down to 4.7 metres with false platforms which provide acoustic conditioning.

At the back of the main room an access stairway leading to the washrooms and the kitchens was installed with a floor surfacing identical to that of the rest of the premises. Iron and brass balustrades, similar to those found at the entrance to the restaurant, frame the stairway.

The entrance to the piano-bar is on the left of the main room, framed by a great arch divided by two symmetrically placed pillars, one of which was part of the original structure of the building, the other added. The lower halves of both pillars are clad with wood and mirrored surfaces.

The exquisite period decoration and the fine detail of the lighting complete the rehabilitation of these premises, which are almost a hundred years old, converting them into the ideal setting for dinners and gatherings.

Projects such as this are outstanding examples of the rehabilitation of antique buildings, following a line of fundamental respect for historical memory, while at the same time applying the criteria of functionality which are necessary for a space that is used by the public, in this case as a restaurant.

A partial view of the glazed gallery. (B2)

149

TAXIM NIGHTPARK

Branson & Coates Architecture

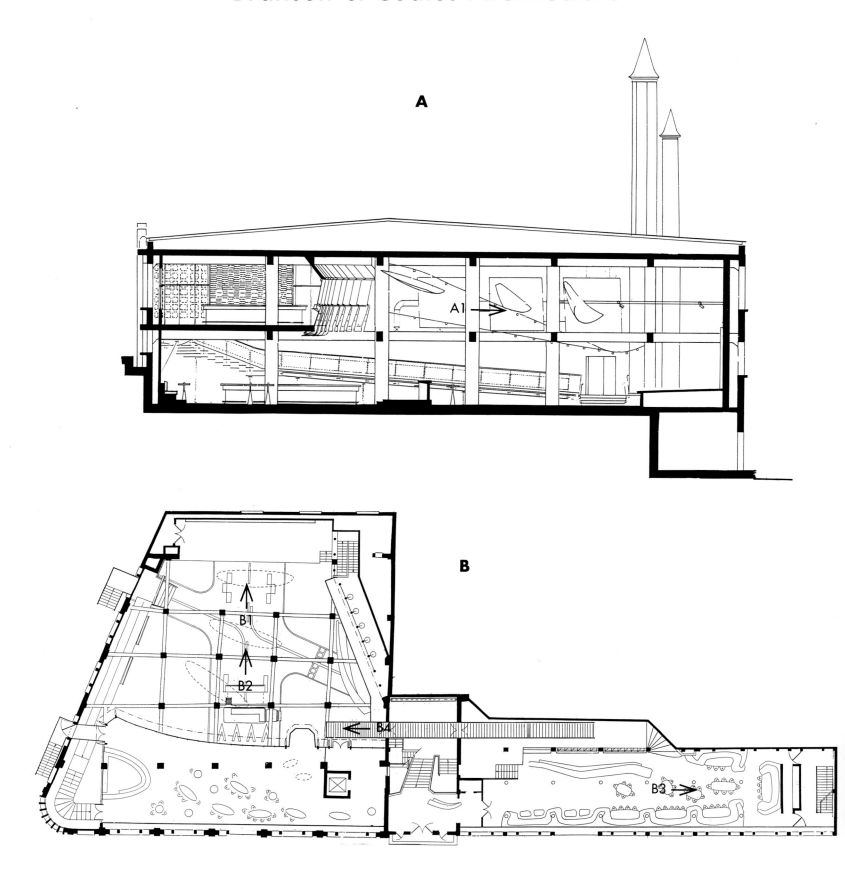

Elevation section of the building. (A)

Floor plan. (B)

The Taxim Nightpark project in Istanbul was conceived by of the desire to transform an old factory building into a recreational multi-space, within the delimitations of innovation and design as applied to leisure premises, similar to those which already existed in Europe, Japan and the United States. The idea of the promoter, Metin Fadillioglu, was to create modern premises with a variety of leisure areas including an elegant restaurant, a large discotheque and various bars and dance areas. A further aim was to bring the Turkish capital up to date in terms of the latest trends in the field of leisure.

The project was successfully completed by Branson & Coates Architecture, a practice set up in 1985 by two British architects Nigel Coates and Doug Branson. They began their professional collaboration after an early stage of their careers spent mainly in education and research, although they did take on the occasional project, and as a team worked on the Metropole Restaurant, the Bohemia Jazz Club and Caffe Bongo, all in London. They became the first British architects to work in the Japanese market completing the Arca di Noe building in Sapporo, in 1988 and the Nishi Azaba Wall commercial complex in Tokyo, in 1990, among many other projects. Their designs for fashion shops have been outstanding, working for such prestigious names as Katherine Hamnett, Jewellery Shop and Jigsaw. They have had exhibitions in Paris, Tokyo, London, Milan and many other cities around the world.

To begin with the architects found that they had to resolve the problems presented by the

External view of Taxim nightpark.

151

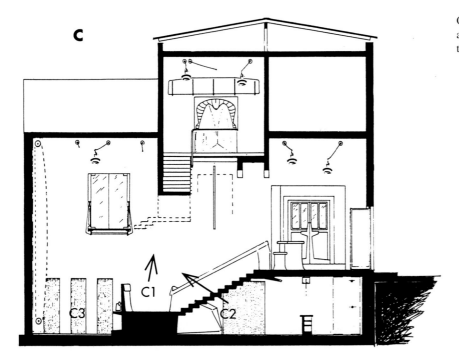

C

On the left, lengthways section of the premises. (C). Below, another lengthways section, this time from the other side of the building. (D)

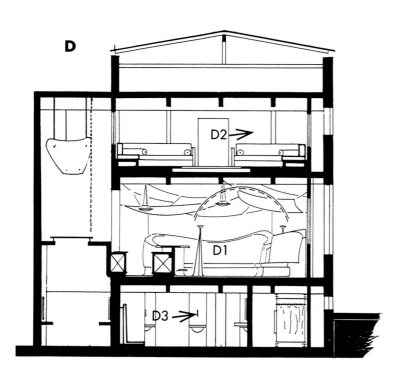

D

original structure of the building, which in its volumetry was characteristic of the constructive language of the manufacturing industry. There was a long and narrow introductory module which opened out onto a much wider space consisting of two and three levels. This run down structure was used as the setting for the idea of the box within a box which established an unusual distinction between the container and the content. The original shell of the old factory became an external skin sheathing a new and luxurious interior which would be clearly visible from the exterior through glazed sections.

The aim, of creating a multi-functional leisure space consisting of various areas led to the need for the redistribution of the interior and the creation of new areas, which would make movement within the space an essential component of the project itself. The communication systems, such as the walkway joining the restaurant and the discotheque, became symbolic references, as did the modern and innovative imagery, the aeronautical motif, and the constant reference to Turkish decorative tradition employed by Branson & Coates. The interior design in general has a scenographic character made manifest by the light-

ing technology, the colour scheme, and the differentiation between the atmospheres of each of the several areas which serve to illustrate the overall framework, dominated by an atmosphere of material deterioration and provoking an expressive and highly suggestive contrast.

In the lobby, which is two stories high, there are two striking and fundamental elements, a glazed metal walkway which on one level links the long narrow module to the main area and an enormous and impressive vertical painting, the work of Mark Prizeman, which greets the visitor as he enters. A complicated framework of stairways link the different levels where the service areas are located. To the right of the entrance there is a restaurant conceived of as an elegant Turkish bazaar in which we find, merely as an anecdote, the longest leather sofa and the longest beaded curtain in the world. The section to the left of the entrance is occupied by a seating and drinking area and the large discotheque space.

The discotheque was conceived as an airfield runway on a reduced scale with striking

On this page, above, a perspective of the upper area of the discotheque with a wall featuring aeronautical motifs, painted by Nigel Coates. (B1). On the left, another view of the discotheque. (A1, B2)

A perspective of the framework of stairways which connect the different levels. (C1)

In the photo on the left, a perspective of the washrooms, on the right, the sofa room on the upper floor and the Stuart Helm mural with motifs taken from classical Turkish symbology. (D2)

codes of imitation and an impressive light show. Certain elements were provided by Turkish Airlines, such as airplane equipment containers, used here as video cabins.

The project for this night park is yet another example of the achievements of Branson & Coates in the field of interior design for leisure premises. It is a magisterial combination of local Turkish methods combined with a highly individual design vision which manages to be both striking and bold.

Firstly, a perspective of the walkway which connects the two main sections of the premises, (B4); followed by, the washrooms on the ground floor, (D3); and finally, a view of the secondary exits also on the ground floor of the building. (C3)

Another perspective of the building, from the exterior, illustrating the contrast between the crudity of the old factory structure and the delicacy of the stained glass with its ornamental motifs.

Below, a view of part of the lower level, showing how in certain areas the crumbling walls and the unpolished floors have been left in their original state. (C2)